The Compact Guide to

Home
Crochet

Learn how to crochet beautiful gifts and homewares that your friends and family will adore! Make beautiful blankets and throws for around the home. Create celebratory vintage-style bunting, greetings cards with a twist, and cute table decorations. Craft handy placemats, coasters, and plant-pot holders to liven up your space, and storage baskets that are as practical as they are pretty. Plus, there are patterns for a brilliant range of baby gifts and amigurumi toys, comfy cushion covers, pet beds for your furry friends, and a whole host of other fun projects to add colour and texture to every room in your home.

sona
BOOKS

First published in the UK 2021 by Sona Books
an imprint of Danann Media Publishing Ltd.

Copy Editor for Danann Tom O'Neill

Designs by Betty Barnden p54,72;
Tash Bentley p48,56,60,76,98,108,118,122;
Monika Cobel p44; Emily Lister p78; Sara Mackin p32,62,64,70,84,126;
Lynne Rowe p30,40,42,66,68,90,94,106; Lesley Stanfield p50;
Louise Watling p100

Styling by Emma Wiltshire
except Anne Hartnett p50; Teresa Conway p78

Photography by Sussie Bell
except Liz McAulay p50; Angela Spain p78; Claire Lloyd Davies p110;
TI-MEDIACONTENT.COM p100

Additional makes by TIMEINCUKCONTENT.COM
p20,28,46,74,80,88,114

CAT NO: SON0582
ISBN: 978-1-915343-36-9

Made in the UAE.

Contents

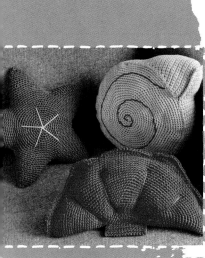

Gifts & Amigurumi

Home

Sweetpea Blanket

In a beautiful spring palette, this blanket is worked
in rows and is the perfect project for beginners

DIFFICULTY

✕ ✕ ✕ ✕

WHAT YOU NEED

- 4mm & 5mm crochet hooks
- Removable stitch markers (optional)
- Washable toy stuffings
- 9mm black safety eyes
- Stylecraft Special DK (100% acrylic)

Colour 1: 2 x 100g (295m) Cream (1005)

Colour 2: 1 x 100g Mid Blue (1019)

Colour 3: 1 x 100g Dark Pink (1241)

Colour 4: 1 x 100g Dark Green (1834)

Colour 5: 1 x 100g Lemon (1020)

Colour 6: 1 x 100g Light Blue (1034)

Colour 7: 1 x 100g Light Pink (1130)

Colour 8: 1 x 100g Light Green (1336)

MEASUREMENTS

Complete blanket measures approximately 89 x 132cm/35 x 52in, including border.

ABBREVIATIONS

Ch, chain; st(s), stitches; dc, double crochet; tr, treble crochet; chsp, chain space; sp, space; yrh, yarn round hook; slst, slip stitch.

PATTERN
TO MAKE

Foundation chain: With 5mm hook and Mid Blue, make 121ch.

Change to 4mm hook.

1st row: 1dc in 2nd ch from hook, [1dc in next ch] to end, turn – 120 sts.

2nd row: 1ch (does not count as a st throughout), [1dc in next st] to end, turn.

3rd row: 1ch, [1dc in next st] to end, turn.

4th row: As 3rd row, changing to Dark Pink on last yrh of last dc, turn.

5th row: 3ch (counts as 1tr throughout), skip st at base of 3ch, [1tr in next st] to end, turn.

6th row: 3ch, [1tr in next st] to end, changing to Cream on last yrh of last tr, turn.

7th and 8th rows: As 3rd and 4th rows, changing to Dark Green on last yrh of last dc of 8th row.

9th row: 1st Granny stripe row: 3ch, 1tr in st at base of 3ch, [skip 2 sts, 3tr in next st] to last 2 sts, skip 1 st, 1tr in last st, turn.

10th row: 2nd Granny stripe row: 3ch, 1tr in st at base of 3ch, [3tr in sp between next 2 tr-groups] to last 2 sts, skip 1 st, 1tr in last st, turn.

11th row: 3rd Granny stripe row: As 10th row, changing to Cream on last yrh of last tr, turn.

12th and 13th rows: As 3rd and 4th rows, changing to Lemon on last yrh of last dc of 13th row, turn.

14th and 15th rows: As 9th and 10th rows.

16th and 17th rows: As 10th and 11th rows, changing to Cream on last yrh of last tr of 17th row, turn.

18th and 19th rows: As 3rd and 4th rows, changing to Light Blue on last yrh of last dc of 19th row, turn.

20th and 21st rows: As 5th and 6th rows, changing to Light Pink on last yrh of last tr of 21st row, turn.

22nd and 23rd rows: As 5th and 6th rows, changing to Cream on last yrh of last tr of 23rd row, turn.

24th and 25th rows: As 3rd and 4th rows, changing to Light Green on last yrh of last dc of 25th row, turn.

26th to 27th rows: As 9th and 10th rows.

28th and 29th rows: As 10th and 11th rows, changing to Cream on last yrh of last tr of 29th row, turn.

30th and 31st rows: As 3rd and 4th rows, changing to Mid Blue on last yrh of last dc of 31st row, turn.

32th to 34th rows: As 9th to 11th rows, changing to Cream on last yrh of last tr of 34th row, turn.

35th and 36th rows: As 3rd and 4th rows, changing to Dark Pink on last yrh of last dc of 36th row, turn.

37th and 38th rows: As 5th and 6th rows, changing to Dark Green on last yrh of last tr of 38th row, turn.

39th and 40th rows: As 5th and 6th rows, changing to Cream on last yrh of last tr of 40th row, turn.

41st row: 1ch, [1dc in next st] to end, turn.

42nd row: As 41st row, changing to Lemon on last yrh of last dc, turn.

43rd row: 1st V-stitch row: 3ch, skip st at base of 3ch, 2tr in next st, [skip next st, 2tr in next st] to last 2 sts, skip next st, 1tr in last st, changing to Light Blue on last yrh of last tr, turn.

44th row: 2nd V-stitch row: 3ch, [2tr in sp between the 2 tr of next 2tr-gp] to last st, 1tr in last st, changing to Light Pink on last yrh of last tr, turn. >

45th row: 3rd V-stitch row: As 44th row, changing to Light Green on last yrh of last tr, turn.

46th row: 4th V-stitch row: As 44th row, changing to Cream on last yrh of last tr, turn.

47th and 48th rows: As 41st and 42nd rows, changing to Mid Blue on last yrh of last dc of 48th row, turn.

49th row: As 43rd row, changing to Dark Pink on last yrh of last tr, turn.

PATTERN NOTES

- The starting chain is worked with a 5mm hook to prevent the first row from being too tight and to make the chains easier to work into. If you prefer, place a removable stitch marker in every 20th ch on your foundation chain, to help keep track of counting. On some rows, the last stitch of the row is the beginning 3ch from the previous row, which is always counted as a stitch. It is really important to finish with a tr in the top of this 3ch as this will keep your edges nice and straight and it will keep your stitch count correct. You may find it helpful to tick each numbered row off as you go along, especially if this is your first big project. Unless stated otherwise, when changing colours, break off the current yarn. To avoid a daunting task, weave in yarn tails as you go along or at the end of each section. Yarn amounts are based on average requirements and are therefore approximate. Instructions in square brackets are worked as stated after 2nd bracket.

50th row: As 44th row, changing to Dark Green on last yrh of last tr, turn.

51st row: As 44th row, changing to Cream on last yrh of last tr, turn.

52nd and 53rd rows: As 41st and 42nd rows, changing to Lemon on last yrh of last dc of 53rd row, turn.

54th row: 3ch, skip st at base of 3ch, [1tr in next st] to end, turn.

55th row: As 54th row, changing to Light Blue on last yrh of last tr, turn.

56th and 57th rows: As 54th and 55th rows, changing to Cream on last yrh of last tr of 57th row, turn.

58th and 59th rows: As 41st and 42nd rows, changing to Light Pink on last yrh of last dc of 59th row, turn.

60th row: As 43rd row, changing to Light Green on last yrh of last tr, turn.

61st row: As 44th row, changing to Mid Blue on last yrh of last tr, turn.

62nd row: As 44th row, changing to Dark Pink on last yrh of last tr, turn.

63rd row: As 44th row, changing to Cream on last yrh of last tr, turn.

64th and 65th rows: As 41st and 42nd rows, changing to Dark Green on last yrh of last dc of 65th row, turn.

66th row: As 43rd row, changing to Lemon on last yrh of last tr, turn.

67th row: As 44th row, changing to Light Blue on last yrh of last tr, turn.

68th row: As 44th row, changing to Cream on last yrh of last tr, turn.

69th and 70th rows: As 41st and 42nd rows, changing to Light Pink on last yrh of last dc of 70th row, turn.

71st and 72nd rows: As 54th and 55th rows, changing to Light Green on last yrh of last tr of 72nd row, turn.

73rd and 74th rows: As 54th and 55th rows, changing to Cream on last yrh of last tr of 74th row, turn.

75th and 76th rows: As 41st and 42nd rows, but changing to Mid Blue on last yrh of last dc of 76th row, turn.

77th row: 1st Granny stripe row: 3ch, 1tr in st at base of 3ch, [skip 2 sts, 3tr in next st] to last 2 sts, skip 1 st, 1tr in last st, turn.

78th row: 2nd Granny stripe row: 3ch, 1tr in st at base of 3ch, [3tr in sp between next 2 tr-groups] to last 2 sts, skip 1 st, 1tr in last st, turn.

79th row: 3rd Granny stripe row: As 78th row, changing to Cream on last yrh of last tr, turn.

80th row: 1ch, [1dc in next st] to end, turn.

81st row: As 80th row, changing to Dark Pink on last yrh of last dc, turn.

82nd and 83rd rows: As 77th and 78th rows.

84th and 85th rows: As 78th and 79th rows, changing to Cream on last yrh of last tr of 85th row, turn.

86th and 87th rows: As 80th and 81st rows, changing to Dark Green on last yrh of last dc of 87th row, turn.

88th row: 3ch, skip st at base of 3ch, [1tr in next st] to end, turn.

89th row: As 88th row, changing to Lemon on last yrh of last tr, turn.

90th and 91st rows: As 88th and 89th rows, changing to Cream on last yrh of last tr of 91st row, turn.

92nd and 93rd rows: As 80th and 81st rows, changing to Light Blue on last yrh of last dc of 93rd row, turn.

94th and 95th rows: As 77th and 78th rows.

96th and 97th rows: As 78th and 79th rows, changing to Cream on last yrh of last tr of 97th row, turn.

98th and 99th rows: As 80th and 81st rows, changing to Light Pink on last yrh of last dc of 99th row, turn.

100th to 102nd rows: As 77th to 79th rows, and change to Cream on last yrh of last tr of 102nd row, turn.

103rd and 104th rows: As 80th and 81st rows, changing to Light Green on last yrh of last dc of 104th row, turn.

105th and 106th rows: As 88th and 89th rows, changing to Mid Blue on last yrh of last tr of 106th row, turn.

107th and 108th rows: As 88th and 89th rows, changing to Cream on last yrh of last tr of 108th row, turn.

109th row: 1ch, [1dc in next st] to end, turn.

110th row: As 109th row, changing to Dark Pink on last yrh of last dc, turn.

111th row: 1st V-stitch row: 3ch, skip st at base of 3ch, 2tr in next st, [skip next st, 2tr in next st] to last 2 sts, skip next st, 1tr in last st, changing to Dark Green on last yrh of last tr, turn.

112th row: 2nd V-stitch row: 3ch, [2tr in sp between the 2 tr of next 2tr-gp] to last st, 1tr in last st, changing to Lemon on last yrh of last tr, turn.

113th row: 3rd V-stitch row: As 112th row, changing to Light Blue on last yrh of last tr, turn.

114th row: 4th V-stitch row: As 112th row, changing to Cream on last yrh of last tr, turn.

115th and 116th rows: As 109th and 110th rows, changing to Light Pink on last yrh of last dc of 116th row, turn.

117th row: As 111th row, changing to Light Green on last yrh of last tr, turn.

118th row: As 112th row, changing to Mid Blue on last yrh of last tr, turn.

119th row: As 112th row, changing to Cream on last yrh of last tr, turn.

120th and 121st rows: As 109th and 110th rows, changing to Dark Pink on last yrh of last dc of 121st row, turn.

122nd row: 3ch, skip st at base of 3ch, [1tr in next st] to end, turn.

123rd row: As 122nd row, changing to Dark Green on last yrh of last tr, turn.

124th and 125th rows: As 122nd and 123rd rows, changing to Cream on last yrh of last tr of 125th row, turn.

126th and 127th rows: As 109th and 110th rows, changing to Lemon on last yrh of last dc of 127th row, turn.

128th row: As 111th row, changing to Light Blue on last yrh of last tr, turn.

129th row: As 112th row, changing to Light Pink on last yrh of last tr, turn.

130th row: As 112th row, changing to Light Green on last yrh of last tr, turn.

131st row: As 112th row, changing to Cream on last yrh of last tr, turn.

132nd and 133rd rows: As 109th and 110th rows, changing to Mid Blue on last yrh of last dc of 110th row, turn.

134th row: As 111th row, changing to Dark Pink on last yrh of last tr, turn.

135th row: As 112th row, changing to Dark Green on last yrh of last tr, turn.

136th row: As 112th row, changing to Cream on last yrh of last tr, turn.

137th and 138th rows: As 109th and 110th rows, changing to Lemon on last yrh of last dc of 138th row, turn.

139th row: As 122nd row, changing to Light Blue on last yrh of last tr, turn.

140th to 143rd rows: As 109th row.

Fasten off.

NOTE

When working the border, especially along the row-ends, work a section at a time and check your tension. If your work is pulling, add a few more trebles evenly spaced; if the work is wavy and loose, decrease the number of trebles along the sides evenly spaced.

Unless stated otherwise, when changing colours, break off the current yarn. To avoid a daunting task, weave in yarn tails as you go along.

With 4mm hook and Cream, hold blanket with Mid Blue foundation ch uppermost and join yarn with slst to right-hand corner. Work along opposite loops of foundation chain and work in rounds that are joined.

1st round: 3ch (counts as 1tr throughout), *[1tr in next st] to next corner, work 3tr in corner st, [1tr in each dc row-end and 2tr in each tr row-end] to next corner, work 3tr in corner st; repeat from * once more, slst in beginning 3ch.

2nd round: 1ch (does not count as a st throughout), *[1dc in next st] to next corner, work 3dc in corner st; repeat from * to end, slst in beginning 1ch.

3rd round: Join Dark Green to st to left of top right corner st. As 2nd round.

4th round: Join Lemon to st to left of top right corner st. As 2nd round.

5th round: Join Light Blue to st to left of top right corner st. As 2nd round.

6th round: Join Light Pink to st to left of top right corner st. As 2nd round.

7th round: Join Cream to st to left of top right corner st. As 2nd round.

8th round: With Cream, 3ch, * [1tr in next st] to next corner, 3tr in corner st; repeat from * to end, slst in beginning 3ch.

9th round: Join Light Green to any st, 1ch, [slst in next st] to end. Fasten off.

Edging round: With wrong side facing, join Cream and work along back of blanket, 3ch (not counted as a st), 1tr in same st at base of beginning 3ch, [slst in next st, 1tr in next st] to end, slst into top of first tr. Fasten off. Neaten your final tails and you are finished. Enjoy snuggling with your beautiful blanket!

Shore Thing

Our set of three lovely shell cushions
will tide you over

*We've opted for a chunky
yarn to make up this set
extra quickly*

DIFFICULTY

✕ ✕ ✕ ✕

WHAT YOU NEED

- 6mm crochet hook
- Removable stitch markers or contrast thread
- Washable toy stuffings
- King Cole Comfort Chunky
  (60% acryllc, 40% nylon)

Fan Cushion:

Colour 1: 3 x 100g (106m) Pink (3192)

Colour 2: Short length Purple (3193)

Spiral Cushion:

Colour 1: 5 x 100g (106m) Blue (427)

Colour 2: Short length Pink (3192)

Star Cushion:

Colour 1: 3 x 100g (106m) Purple (3193)

Colour 2: Short length Blue (427)

MEASUREMENTS

Fan Cushion: Approximately 42cm/16½in wide and 25cm/10in deep.

Spiral Cushion: Approximately 40cm/15¾in at widest point and 30cm/11¾in deep.

Star Cushion: Approximately 36cm/14in across.

TENSION

Tension is not critical. Use a smaller hook size than recommended for your yarn, so that the toy stuffing is not visible through the stitches.

ABBREVIATIONS

Ch, chain; st(s), stitches; dc, double crochet; tr, treble crochet; htr, half treble crochet; dtr, double treble crochet; dc2tog, double crochet 2 sts together (to decrease 1 st) thus, [insert hook Into next st, yrh, and pull a loop through] twice, yrh and pull through all 3 loops on hook; yrh, yarn round hook.

FAN CUSHION
MAIN BODY

1st round: With 6mm hook and Pink, make a slip ring as follows, wind yarn round index finger of left hand to form a ring, insert hook into ring, yarn round hook and pull through, 1ch, (does not count as a st) work 6dc in ring, pull end of yarn tightly to close ring – 6 sts.

Place st marker in last st, and move this up at end of each round.

2nd round: [2dc in next st] 6 times – 12 sts.

3rd round: [2dc in next st, 1dc in next st] 6 times – 18 sts.

4th round: [2dc in next st, 1dc in each of next 2 sts] 6 times – 24 sts.

5th round: [2dc in next st, 1dc in each of next 3 sts] 6 times – 30 sts.

6th round: [2dc in next st, 1dc in each of next 4 sts] 6 times – 36 sts.

7th round: [2dc in next st, 1dc in each of next 5 sts] 6 times – 42 sts.

8th round: [2dc in next st, 1dc in each of next 6 sts] 6 times – 48 sts.

9th round: [2dc in next st, 1dc in each of next 7 sts] 6 times – 54 sts.

10th round: [2dc in next st, 1dc in each of next 8 sts] 6 times – 60 sts.

11th round: [2dc in next st, 1dc in each of next 9 sts] 6 times – 66 sts.

12th round: [2dc in next st, 1dc in each of next 10 sts] 6 times – 72 sts.

13th round: [2dc in next st, 1dc in each of next 11 sts] 6 times – 78 sts.

14th round: [2dc in next st, 1dc in each of next 12 sts] 6 times – 84 sts.

15th round: [2dc in next st, 1dc in each of next 13 sts] 6 times – 90 sts.

16th round: [2dc in next st, 1dc in each of next 14 sts] 6 times – 96 sts.

17th round: [2dc in next st, 1dc in each of next 15 sts] 6 times – 102 sts.

18th round: [2dc in next st, 1dc in each of next 16 sts] 6 times – 108 sts.

19th round: [2dc in next st, 1dc in each of next 17 sts] 6 times – 114 sts.

20th round: [2dc in next st, 1dc in each of next 18 sts] 6 times – 120 sts.

21st round: [2dc in next st, 1dc in each of next 19 sts] 6 times – 126 sts.

22nd round: [2dc in next st, 1dc in each of next 20 sts] 6 times – 132 sts.

23rd round: [2dc in next st, 1dc in each of next 21 sts] 6 times – 138 sts.

24th round: [2dc in next st, 1dc in each of next 22 sts] 6 times – 144 sts. **

25th round: [2dc in next st, 1dc in each of next 23 sts] 6 times – 150 sts.

26th round: [2dc in next st, 1dc in each of next 24 sts] 6 times – 156 sts.

27th round: [2dc in next st, 1dc in each of next 25 sts] 6 times – 162 sts.

28th round: [2dc in next st, 1dc in each of next 26 sts] 6 times – 168 sts.

29th round: [2dc in next st, 1dc in each of next 27 sts] 6 times – 174 sts.

30th round: [2dc in next st, 1dc in each of next 28 sts] 6 times –180 sts.

31st round: [2dc in next st, 1dc in each of next 29 sts] 6 times – 186 sts.

32nd round: [2dc in next st, 1dc in each of next 30 sts] 6 times – 192 sts.

Do not break off yarn.

Fold circle in half and working through both sets of edge stitches to join, and stuffing as you work, continue as follows,

Row 1: Skip 1 dc, [1dc in next st, working through both thicknesses] 95 times, turn – 95 sts.

Row 2: 1ch (does not count as a st), starting in same st at base of 1ch, [1dc in next st, 1htr in each of next 2 sts, 1tr in each of next 4 sts, 1dtr in each of next 5 sts, 1tr in each of next 4 sts, 1htr in each of next 2 sts, 1dc in next st] 5 times. Fasten off.

BOTTOM TAB

With Pink, make 15ch.

1st row: 1dc in 2nd ch from hook, [1dc in next ch] to end, turn – 14 sts.

2nd to 12th rows: 1ch (does not count as a st), [1dc in next st] to end. Fasten off. Fold in half, bringing together the 1st and 12th rows, and sew around edges to join. Sew one long edge of tab to centre of straight edge of cushion.

With Purple, thread four long, vertical straight sts through both sides of cushion, equally distributed around the fan shape, using photo as a guide. Pull yarn tight to create a quilted effect.

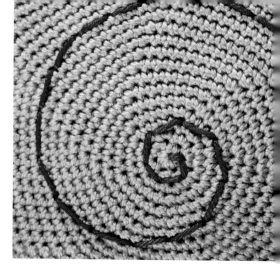

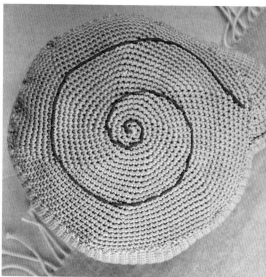

SPIRAL CUSHION
FRONT AND BACK (MAKE 2 ALIKE)

With Blue, work as given for Fan Cushion to **.

Fasten off. With Pink, starting from the centre and working towards the outside of the cushion, embroider a spiral on both sides with back stitch, using photo as a guide.

SIDE

With Blue, make 33ch.

1st row: 1dc in 2nd ch from hook, [1dc in next ch] to end, turn – 32 sts.

2nd row: 1ch (does not count as a st throughout), [1dc in next st] to end, turn.

3rd row: 1ch, dc2tog, [1dc in next st] to last 2 sts, dc2tog, turn – 2 sts decreased.

4th to 25th rows: Repeat 2nd and 3rd rows, 11 times more – 8 sts.

Use the leftover yarn for the embroidery

26th to 169th rows: 1ch [1dc in next st] to end, turn (marking each end of 157th row with removable st markers or contrast thread).

Fasten off.

Bring 1st row around and line up each end of 1st row with markers on 157th row. Pin edge of 1st row to edges of rectangular tab created by 157th to 169th rows. Rejoin Blue and work 1ch (does not count as a st), [1dc in next st, working through both thicknesses] along seam. Fasten off.

Whip stitch the edges of front and back to side section, stuffing as you go.

All three cushions use double crochet

10th round: [2dc in next st, 1dc in each of next 8 sts] 5 times – 50 sts.

11th round: [2dc in next st, 1dc in each of next 9 sts] 5 times – 55 sts.

12th round: [2dc in next st, 1dc in each of next 10 sts] 5 times – 60 sts.

13th round: [2dc in next st, 1dc in each of next 11 sts] 5 times – 65 sts.

14th round: [2dc in next st, 1dc in each of next 12 sts] 5 times – 70 sts.

15th round: [2dc in next st, 1dc in each of next 13 sts] 5 times – 75 sts.

16th round: [2dc in next st, 1dc in each of next 14 sts] 5 times – 80 sts.

17th round: [2dc in next st, 1dc in each of next 15 sts] 5 times – 85 sts.

18th round: [2dc in next st, 1dc in each of next 16 sts] 5 times – 90 sts.

Fasten off the back but do not fasten off the front.

Continue to make the points of the star, working in rounds and connecting the front and back pieces to form seamless points. Hold front and back pieces with wrong sides together.

*** 19th round: [1dc in next st] 18 times on front piece, [1dc in next st] 18 times on back piece – 36 sts.

Place st marker in last st, and move this up at end of each round.

20th round: [1dc in next st] to end.

21st round: [Dc2tog, 1dc in each of next 4 sts] 6 times – 30 sts.

22nd and 23rd rounds: [1dc in next st] to end. 24th round: [Dc2tog, 1dc in each of next 3 sts] 6 times – 24 sts.

25th and 26th rounds: [1dc in next st] to end.

27th round: [Dc2tog, 1dc in each of next 2 sts] 6 times –18 sts.

28th and 29th rounds: [1dc in next st] to end. 30th round: [Dc2tog, 1dc in next st] 6 times – 12 sts.

31st round: [1dc in next st] to end.

32nd round: [Dc2tog] 6 times – 6 sts.

33rd round: [Dc2tog] 3 times – 3 sts.

Fasten off.

*** Repeat from *** to ***, 5 times more, for each of the 5 points around the front and back pieces, stuffing as you go. Always begin in the next unworked dc of 18th round.

With Blue, embroider star detail on front and back, using photo as a guide. With Purple, sew up gaps between the points.

STARFISH CUSHION
FRONT AND BACK (MAKE 2 ALIKE)

1st round: With 6mm hook and Purple, make a slip ring as follows, wind yarn round index finger of left hand to form a ring, insert hook into ring, yarn round hook and pull through, 1ch, (does not count as a st) work 5dc in ring, pull end of yarn tightly to close ring – 5 sts.

Place st marker in last st, and move this up at end of each round.

2nd round: [2dc in next st] 5 times – 10 sts

3rd round: [2dc in next st, 1dc in next st] 5 times – 15 sts.

4th round: [2dc in next st, 1dc in each of next 2 sts] 5 times – 20 sts.

5th round: [2dc in next st, 1dc in each of next 3 sts] 5 times – 25 sts.

6th round: [2dc in next st, 1dc in each of next 4 sts] 5 times – 30 sts.

7th round: [2dc in next st, 1dc in each of next 5 sts] 5 times – 35 sts.

8th round: [2dc in next st, 1dc in each of next 6 sts] 5 times – 40 sts.

9th round: [2dc in next st, 1dc in each of next 7 sts] 5 times – 45 sts.

PATTERN NOTES

• Most pieces are worked in a continuous spiral without joining each round. Use a removable st marker to mark the last st of the round and move it up as you work. Yarn amounts are based on average requirements and are therefore approximate. Instructions in square brackets are worked as stated after 2nd bracket.

Staying Neutral

Lighten up your home with stunning crochet
projects in pale neutral shades

PATTERN NOTES

• Yarn amounts are based on average
requirements and are therefore approximate.
Instructions in square brackets are worked
as stated after 2nd bracket.

DIFFICULTY

✕ ✕ ✕ ✕

WHAT YOU NEED

• 2.5mm crochet hook
• DMC Petra 5 (100% cotton)
  Colour: 4 x 100g (400m) Putty (54003)

MEASUREMENTS

Approximately 106 x 106cm/41¾ x 41¾in

TENSION

Each motif measures approximately 16 x 16cm, using 2.5mm hook.

ABBREVIATIONS

Ch, chain; st(s), stitch(es); dc, double crochet; tr, treble crochet; slst, slip st; chsp(s), chain space(s); yrh, yarn round hook; tr4tog, [yrh, insert hook in next st, yrh and pull through, yrh and pull through first 2 loops on hook] 4 times, yrh and pull through all 5 loops on hook; tr5tog, [yrh, insert hook in next st, yrh and pull through, yrh and pull through first 2 loops on hook] 5 times, yrh and pull through all 6 loops on hook.

TABLECLOTH
FIRST ROW OF MOTIFS

First motif: *** With 2.5mm hook, make 8ch and join with a slst in first ch to form a ring.

1st round: 1ch (counts as 1dc), 15dc in ring, slst in beginning 1ch – 16 sts.

2nd round: 7ch (counts as 1tr and 4ch), miss next st, [1tr in next st, 4ch, miss next st] 7 times, slst in 3rd of beginning 7ch – 8 4-chsps.

3rd round: Slst in first chsp, 3ch (counts as 1tr here and throughout), 4tr in same chsp, 1ch, [5tr in next chsp, 1ch] 7 times, slst in top of beginning 3ch – 8 5tr-groups and 8 1-chsps.

4th round: 3ch, 1tr in same st at base of 3ch, 1tr in each of next 3 tr, 2tr in next tr, 3ch, [miss next 1-chsp, 2tr in next tr, 1tr in each of next 3 tr, 2tr in next tr, 3ch] 7 times, slst in top of beginning 3ch.

5th round: Slst in next tr, 2ch, tr4tog, 3ch, miss next st, work [1tr, 3ch and 1tr] all in next chsp, 3ch, *miss next st, tr5tog, 3ch, miss next st, work [1tr, 3ch and 1tr] all in next chsp, 3ch; repeat from * 6 times more, slst in top of tr4tog.

6th round: Slst in each of next 3 ch and first tr, 6ch (counts as 1tr and 3ch throughout), 1tr in same st at base of 6ch, *3ch, miss next chsp, work [1tr, 3ch and 1tr] all in next tr, 4ch, miss next chsp and next tr5tog, 1tr in next chsp, 3tr in next tr, work [1tr, 3ch and 1tr] all in next chsp, 3tr in next tr, 1tr in next chsp, 4ch, miss next tr5tog and chsp, work [1tr, 3ch and 1tr] all in next tr; repeat from * 3 times more, omitting [1tr, 3ch and 1tr] at end of last repeat, slst in 3rd of beginning 6ch.

7th round: 6ch, 1tr in same st at base of 6ch, *miss next 3-chsp and next tr, work [1tr, 3ch and 1tr] in next 3-chsp, miss next tr and 3-chsp, work [1tr, 3ch and 1tr] all in next tr, 5ch, miss next 4-chsp, tr5tog, 3ch, 5tr in next 3-chsp, 3ch, tr5tog, 5ch, miss next 4-chsp, work [1tr, 3ch and 1tr] all in next tr; repeat from * 3 times more, omitting [1tr, 3ch and 1tr] at end of last repeat, slst in 3rd of beginning 6ch.

8th round: 6ch, 1tr in same st at base of 6ch, *miss next 3-chsp, [1tr in next tr, 3ch, 1tr in next tr, miss next 3-chsp] twice, work [1tr, 3ch and 1tr] all in next tr, 5ch, miss next 5-chsp and tr5tog, 1tr in next chsp, 5ch, tr5tog, 5ch, 1tr in next 3-chsp, 5ch, miss next tr5tog and 5-chsp, work [1tr, 3ch and 1tr] all in next tr; repeat from * 3 times more, omitting [1tr, 3ch and 1tr] at end of last repeat, slst in 3rd of beginning 6ch.

9th round: 6ch, 1tr in same st at base of 6ch, *miss next 3-chsp, [1tr in next tr, 3ch, 1tr in next tr, miss next 3-chsp] 3 times, work [1tr, 3ch and 1tr] all in next tr, 7ch, miss next 5-chsp and next tr, 1dc in next 5-chsp, 9ch, miss tr5tog, 1dc in next 5-chsp, 7ch, miss next tr and 5-chsp, work [1tr, 3ch and 1tr] all in next tr; repeat from * 3 times more, omitting [1tr, 3ch and 1tr] at end of last repeat, slst in 3rd of beginning 6ch. ***

10th round: 6ch, 1tr in same st at base of 6ch, *miss next 3-chsp, [1tr in next tr, 3ch, 1tr in next tr, miss next 3-chsp] 4 times, work [1tr, 3ch and 1tr] all in next tr, 7ch, miss next 7-chsp and next dc, work [5tr, 11ch and 5tr] all in next 9-chsp, 7ch, miss next dc and 7-chsp, work [1tr, 3ch and 1tr] all in next tr; repeat from * 3 times more, omitting [1tr, 3ch and 1tr] at end of last repeat, slst in 3rd of beginning 6ch. Fasten off.

Second motif: Work as given for first motif from *** to ***.

Always join motifs from left to right.

10th joining round: With wrong sides together and current motif facing, work 3ch and slst in corresponding tr on previous motif, 1ch, 1dc in first 3-chsp on previous motif, 1ch, 1tr in base of first 3ch on current motif, miss next 3-chsp on current motif, [1tr in next tr on current motif, 1ch, 1dc in next 3-chsp on previous motif, 1ch, 1tr in next tr on current motif, miss next 3-chsp on current motif] 4 times, 1tr in next tr on current motif, 1ch, 1dc in next 3-chsp on previous motif, 1ch, 1tr in same place as last tr worked on current motif, slst in next tr on previous motif, 7ch, miss next 7-chsp and next dc on current motif, 5tr in next 9-chsp on current motif, 5ch, slst in corresponding 11-chsp on previous motif, 5ch, 5tr in same 9-chsp on current motif as last 5tr, continue on current motif, 7ch, miss next dc and 7-chsp, work [1tr, 3ch and 1tr] all in next tr, *miss next 3-chsp, [1tr in next tr, 3ch, 1tr in next tr, miss next 3-chsp] 4 times, work [1tr, 3ch and 1tr] all in next tr, 7ch, miss next 7-chsp and next dc **, work [5tr, 11ch and 5tr] all in next 9-chsp, 7ch, miss next dc and 7-chsp, work [1tr, 3ch and 1tr] all in next tr; repeat from * once more, then repeat from * to ** again, 5tr in next 9-chsp on current motif, 5ch, 1dc in corresponding 11-chsp on previous motif, 5ch, 5tr in same 9-chsp on current motif as last 5tr, 7ch, miss next dc and 7-chsp on current motif, slst in top of 3ch at beginning of current motif.

Fasten off and neaten all ends.

Third to sixth motifs: Working as given for second motif, make and join another 4 motifs to last 2 motifs to complete first row of 6 motifs.

SECOND ROW OF MOTIFS

Seventh motif: Work as given for first motif from *** to ***.

10th joining round: With wrong side of current motif facing wrong side of first motif, work as given for 10th joining round of second motif.

Eighth motif: Work as given for first motif from *** to ***.

10th joining round: With wrong side of current motif facing wrong side of second motif, work 3ch, *slst in top of corresponding tr on previous motif, 1ch, 1dc in next 3-chsp on previous motif, 1ch, 1tr in same place as last tr worked on current motif, miss next 3-chsp on current motif, [1tr in next tr on current motif, 1ch, 1dc in next 3-chsp on previous motif, 1ch, 1tr in next tr on current motif, miss next 3-chsp on current motif] 4 times, 1tr in next tr on current motif, 1ch, 1dc in next 3-chsp on previous motif, 1ch, 1tr in same place as last tr worked on current motif, slst in next tr on previous motif, 7ch, miss next 7-chsp and next dc on current motif, 5tr in next 9-chsp on current motif, 5ch, slst in corresponding 11-chsp on previous motif, 5ch, 5tr in same 9-chsp on current motif as last 5tr, 7ch, miss next dc and 7-chsp on current motif, 1tr in next tr on current motif; repeat from * once more, continue on current motif, **3ch, 1tr in same place as last tr worked, miss next 3-chsp, [1tr in next tr, 3ch, 1tr in next tr, miss next 3-chsp] 4 times, work [1tr, 3ch and 1tr] all in next tr, 7ch, miss next 7-chsp and next dc**, work [5tr, 11ch and 5tr] all in next 9-chsp, 7ch, miss next dc and 7-chsp, 1tr in next st; repeat from ** to **

once more, 5tr in next 9-chsp on current motif, 5ch, slst in corresponding 11-chsp on previous motif, 5ch, 5tr in same 9-chsp on current motif as last 5tr, 7ch, miss next dc and 7-chsp on current motif, slst in 3rd of 3ch at beginning of current motif. Fasten off and neaten ends.

Ninth to twelfth motifs: Working as given for eighth motif, make and join another 4 motifs to complete 2nd row of 6 motifs.

TO MAKE UP

Make and join another 4 rows each of 6 motifs to first two rows to make a 6 x 6 motif square tablecloth.

Edging: 1st round: With right side facing and with 2.5mm hook, join in yarn to left side of 11-chsp at any corner of tablecloth and work 1ch and 1dc in same place as join, *5ch, miss next 2 tr, 1tr in next tr, 5ch, miss next 2 tr, 1dc in next 7-chsp, [5ch, 1dc in next 3-chsp] 6 times, 5ch, 1dc in next 7-chsp, 5ch, miss next 2 tr, 1tr in next tr, 5ch, miss next 2 tr, 1dc in 11-chsp at corner of motif, 5ch, 1dc in join between motifs, 5ch, 1dc in 11-chsp at corner of next motif; repeat from * 4 times more, 5ch, miss next 2 tr, 1tr in next tr, 5ch, miss next 2 tr, 1dc in next 7-chsp, [5ch, 1dc in next 3-chsp] 6 times, 5ch, 1dc in next 7-chsp, 5ch, miss next 2 tr, 1tr in next tr, 5ch, miss next 2 tr, 1dc in 11-chsp at corner of tablecloth, [5ch, 1dc in same place as last dc] 3 times**, repeat from * to ** 3 times more, omitting 1dc at end of last repeat, slst in first dc.

2nd round: Slst along to centre of first 5-chsp, 1ch, 1dc in same 5-chsp, *[5ch, 1dc in next 5-chsp] along side, ending 5ch, 1dc in centre 5-chsp at corner, 5ch, 1dc in same place as last dc**; repeat from * to ** 3 times more, 5ch, 1dc in last 5-chsp, 5ch, slst in first dc.

3rd round: Work as given for 2nd round to **, then work as given for 2nd round from * to ** 3 times more, [5ch, 1dc in next 5-chsp] twice, 5ch, slst in first dc.

4th round: Work as given for 2nd round to **, then work as given for 2nd round from * to ** 3 times more, [5ch, 1dc in next 5-chsp] 3 times, 5ch, slst in first dc.

5th round: Slst along to centre of next 5-chsp, 1ch, 1dc in same 5-chsp, *[11ch, 1dc in next 5-chsp] along side, ending 11ch, 1dc in corner 5-chsp, 11ch, 1dc in same place as last dc; repeat from * 3 times more, [11ch, 1dc in next 5-chsp] 4 times, 11ch, slst in first dc.

6th round: Slst along to centre of next 11-chsp, 1ch, 1dc in same 11-chsp, *[4ch, 1dc in next 11-chsp] along side, ending 4ch, 1dc 11-chsp at corner, 4ch, 1dc in same place as last dc; repeat from * 3 times more, [4ch, 1dc in next 11-chsp] 5 times, 4ch, slst in first dc.

7th round: Slst in first 4-chsp, 1ch, work [2dc, 3ch and 2dc] all in same place as slst, *work [2dc, 3ch and 2dc] all in next 4-chsp*; repeat from * to * to corner 4-chsp, work [3dc, 3ch and 3dc] all in corner 4-chsp**; repeat from * to ** 3 times more, then repeat from * to * 6 times, slst in first dc.

Fasten off and neaten ends.

PATTERN NOTES

• When working around the post of a stitch, insert hook from the back or front as indicated, underneath the post of the stitch and not into the top of the st, yarn round hook and pull back through, then complete as a standard treble crochet. Yarn amounts are based on average requirements and are therefore approximate. Instructions in square brackets are worked as stated after 2nd bracket.

DIFFICULTY ✂ ✂ ✂ ✂

WHAT YOU NEED

• 4mm & 4.5mm crochet hooks
• King Cole Cottonsoft DK (100% cotton))
  Colour: 4 x 100g (210m) Oyster (742)

MEASUREMENTS

Approximately 41 x 76.5cm/16 x 30in, excluding fringe.

TENSION

19 stitches and 12 rows, to 10 x 10cm, over pattern, using 4.5mm hook.

ABBREVIATIONS

Ch, chain; st(s), stitch(es); tr, treble crochet; htr, half treble crochet; trfp, treble front post thus, insert hook from the front around the post of the next treble and work a treble crochet; trbp, treble back post thus, insert hook from the back around the post of the next treble and work a treble crochet; dc, double crochet.

BATHMAT

With 4mm hook, make 80ch.

Foundation row: 1tr in 4th ch from hook (counts as 2 sts), [1tr in next ch] to end – 78 sts.

Change to 4.5mm hook.

1st row (right side): 2ch (counts as 1htr), 1trfp in each of next 4 tr, [1trbp in each of next 4 tr, 1trfp in each of next 4 tr]   9 times, 1htr in top of beginning 2ch from previous row, turn.

2nd row: 2ch (counts as 1htr), 1trbp in each of next 4 tr, [1trfp in each of next   4 tr, 1trbp in each of next 4 tr] 9 times, 1htr in top of beginning 2ch from previous row, turn.

3rd row: As 1st row.

4th row: As 2nd row.

5th row: As 2nd row.

6th row: As 1st row.

7th row: As 2nd row.

8th row: As 1st row.

Last 8 rows form pattern. Pattern another 84 rows. Do not fasten off.

Edging: With right side facing and with 4mm hook, work 1ch (does not count as a st), [1dc in next st] to end of row, 3dc in corner, continue to work dc edging evenly around end sts of each pattern block (making sure the edging stays flat and does not flute), 3dc in next corner. Work remaining edges to match, ending with 3dc in last corner, slst in first dc and fasten off.

Fringe: From remaining yarn, cut 20cm lengths – 8 strands for each of 20 tassels. With wrong side facing, insert hook between centre 2 stitches of 1st row of first block, hook folded 8 strands of yarn and pull partway through to create a loop. With hook, catch the free ends and pull them through the loop made. Tug ends to tighten knot. Make tassels in alternate blocks to the end and repeat on other side of mat. Trim the tassels.

DIFFICULTY ✂ ✂ ✂ ✂

WHAT YOU NEED

• 3mm crochet hook
• a cushion pad approximately 36cm/14in diameter
• Sirdar Cotton DK (100% cotton)
  Colour: 2 x 100g (212m) Parchment (537)

MEASUREMENTS

To fit 36cm/14in diameter cushion.

TENSION

22 stitches and 12 rows, to 10 x 10cm, over treble crochet, using 3mm hook.

ABBREVIATIONS

Ch, chain; st(s), stitch(es); dc, double crochet; tr, treble crochet; yrh, yarn round hook; pc, popcorn st thus, work 5tr in next st, remove hook, insert hook in top of first of these 5tr, then back into loop of last of these 5tr and pull loop through first tr, yrh and pull through loop on hook; slst, slip stitch; chsp(s), chain space(s).

CIRCLE CUSHION
BACK

1st round: With 3mm hook, make a slip ring as follows, wind yarn round index finger of left hand to form a ring, insert hook into ring, yrh and pull through, 1ch (does not count as a st), work 11dc in ring, pull end of yarn tightly to close ring, slst in 1st dc – 11 sts.

2nd round: 3ch (counts as 1tr throughout), 2tr in same st at base of 3ch, [3tr in next st] to end, slst in top of beginning 3ch – 33 sts.

3rd round: 3ch, [1tr in next st] to end, slst in top of beginning 3ch.

4th round: 3ch, 1tr in same st at base of 3ch, [2tr in next st] to end, slst in top of beginning 3ch – 66 sts.

5th round: As 3rd round.

6th round: 3ch, 1tr in same st at base of 3ch, 1tr in each of next 5 sts, [2tr in next st, 1tr in each of next 5 sts] to end, slst in top of beginning 3ch – 77 sts.

7th round: 3ch, 1tr in same st at base of 3ch, 1tr in each of next 6 sts, [2tr in next st, 1tr in each of next 6 sts] to end, slst in top of beginning 3ch – 88 sts.

8th to 15th rounds: Continue working as before, working 1tr more between increases on each successive repeat – 176 sts.

16th round: As 3rd round.

17th round: 3ch, pc in next st, [1tr in next st, pc in next st] to end, slst in top of beginning 3ch.

18th round: 3ch, [1tr in next st] to end, slst in top of beginning 3ch. Fasten off.

FRONT

1st round: Work as given for 1st round of back – 11 sts.

2nd round: 3ch, 1tr in same st at base of 3ch, [2tr in next st] to end, slst in topof beginning 3ch – 22 sts.

3rd round: 3ch, 1tr in same st at base of 3ch, 1tr in next st, [2tr in next st, 1tr in next st] to end, slst in top of beginning 3ch – 33 sts.

4th round: 3ch, 1tr in same st at base of 3ch, 1tr in each of next 2 sts, [2tr in next st, 1tr in each of next 2 sts] to end, slst in top of beginning 3ch – 44 sts.

5th round: 3ch, pc in next st, [1tr in next st, pc in next st] to end, slst in top of beginning 3ch.

6th round: 3ch, pc in next st (this is a pc), 1tr in next st, pc in next st, *[1tr, 3ch, 1tr] all in next st, pc in next st, 1tr in next st, pc in next st;

repeat from * 9 times more, 1tr in same st at base of 3ch at beginning, 3ch, slst in top of beginning 3ch – 55 sts and 11 3-chsps.

7th round: Slst in next st (this is a pc), 3ch (counts as 1tr), 4tr in same st at base of 3ch, then complete as given for pc, 1tr in next st, pc in next st (this is a pc), 3ch, miss next st, 1dc in next 3-chsp, 3ch, miss next st, *pc in next st, 1tr in next st, pc in next st, 3ch, miss next st, 1dc in next 3-chsp, 3ch, miss next st; repeat from * 9 times more, slst in top of beginning 3ch – 44 sts and 22 3-chsps.

8th round: Slst in next st (this is a pc), 3ch (counts as 1tr), pc in next st, 1tr in next st, 3ch, 1dc in next 3-chsp, 3ch, 1dc in next 3-chsp, 3ch, *1tr in next st, pc in next st, 1tr in next st, 3ch, 1dc in next 3-chsp, 3ch, 1dc in next 3-chsp, 3ch; repeat from * 9 times more, slst in top of beginning 3ch – 55 sts and 33 3-chsps.

9th round: Slst in next st (this is a pc), 3ch (counts as 1tr), 4tr in same st at base of 3ch, then complete as given for pc, 3ch, miss next st, [1dc in next 3-chsp, 3ch] 3 times, *miss next st, pc in next st, 3ch, miss next st, [1dc in next 3-chsp, 3ch] 3 times; repeat from * 9 times more, slst in top of beginning 3ch – 44 sts and 44 3-chsps.

10th round: Slst in next st (this is a pc), 3ch (counts as 1tr), 1tr in next 3-chsp, 1tr in next st, [2tr in next 3-chsp, 1tr in next st] twice, 1tr in next 3-chsp, *[1tr, 3ch, 1tr] all in next st, 1tr in next 3-chsp, 1tr in next st, [2tr in next 3-chsp, 1tr in next st] twice, 1tr in next 3-chsp; repeat from * 9 times more, 1tr in same st at base of 3ch at beginning, 3ch, slst in top of beginning 3ch – 121 sts and 11 3-chsps.

11th round: Slst in next st (this is a tr, not a 3ch), 3ch (counts as 1tr), 4tr in same st at base of 3ch, then complete as given for pc, 1tr in each of next 7 sts, *pc in next st, 3ch, miss next st, 1dc in next 3-chsp, 3ch, miss next st, pc in next st, 1tr in each of next 7 sts; repeat from * 9 times more, pc in next st, 3ch, miss next st, 1dc in next 3-chsp, 3ch, slst in top of beginning 3ch – 110 sts and 22 3-chsps.

12th round: Slst in next 2 sts (a pc then a tr), 3ch (counts as 1tr), 4tr in same st at base of 3ch, then complete as given for pc, 1tr in each of next 5 sts, *pc in next st, 3ch, miss next st, [1dc in next 3-chsp, 3ch] twice, miss next st, pc in next st, 1tr in each of next 5 sts; repeat from * 9 times more, pc in next st, 3ch, miss next st, [1dc in next 3-chsp, 3ch] twice, slst in top of beginning 3ch – 99 sts and 33 3-chsps.

13th round: Slst in next 2 sts (a pc then a tr), 3ch (counts as 1tr), 4tr in same st at base of 3ch, then complete as given for pc, 1tr in each of

The bobble effect ~~~~ ~~th a popcorn stitch in ~~~~ trebles

PATTERN NOTES

• The cushion cover is slightly smaller than the cushion pad and will stretch to fit snugly. Yarn amounts are based on average requirements and are therefore approximate. Instructions in square brackets are worked as stated after 2nd bracket.

next 3 sts, *pc in next st, 3ch, miss next st, [1dc in next 3-chsp, 3ch] 3 times, miss next st, pc in next st, 1tr in each of next 3 sts; repeat from * 9 times more, pc in next st, 3ch, miss next st, [1dc in next 3-chsp, 3ch] 3 times, slst in top of beginning 3ch – 88 sts and 44 3-chsps.

14th round: Slst in next 2 sts (a pc then a tr), 3ch (counts as 1tr), 4tr in same st at base of 3ch, then complete as given for pc, 1tr in next st, pc in next st, 3ch, miss next st, [1dc in next 3-chsp, 3ch] 4 times, *miss next st, pc in next st, 1tr in next st, pc in next st, 3ch, miss next st, [1dc in next 3-chsp, 3ch] 4 times; repeat from * 9 times more, slst in top of beginning 3ch – 77 sts and 55 3-chsps.

15th round: Slst in next 2 sts (a pc then a tr), 3ch (counts as 1tr), 4tr in same st at base of 3ch, then complete as given for pc, 3ch, miss next st, [1dc in next 3-chsp, 3ch] 5 times, *miss next st, pc in next st, 3ch, miss next st, [1dc in next 3-chsp, 3ch] 5 times; repeat from * 9 times more, slst in top of beginning 3ch – 66 sts and 66 3-chsps.

16th round: Slst in next st (this is a pc), 3ch (counts as 1tr), 1tr in next 3-chsp, 1tr in next st, [2tr in next 3-chsp, 1tr in next st] 4 times, 1tr in next 3-chsp, *1tr in next st, 1tr in next 3-chsp, 1tr in next st, [2tr in next 3-chsp, 1tr in next st] 4 times, 1tr in next 3-chsp; repeat from * 9 times more, slst in top of beginning 3ch – 176 sts.

17th and 18th rounds: Work as given for 17th and 18th rounds of back. Fasten off.

TO MAKE UP

Join back and front pieces together, leaving an opening. Insert a suitably sized cushion pad into the case and join opening.

DIFFICULTY ✕ ✕ ✕ ✕

WHAT YOU NEED
• 3mm crochet hook
• Sirdar Cotton DK (100% cotton)
  Colour: 14 x 100g (212m) Light Taupe (504)

MEASUREMENTS
Approximately 180 x 180cm/71 x 71in, excluding edging.

TENSION
For each individual square, 1st to 13th rows measure 16 x 16cm, using 3mm hook.

ABBREVIATIONS
Ch, chain; dc, double crochet; tr, treble crochet; slst, slip stitch; sp, space; chsp(s), chain space(s)

BEDSPREAD
FIRST STRIP

First square: With 3mm hook, make 44ch.

1st row (right side): 1tr in 8th ch from hook (counts as 1tr, 2-chsp, 1tr), [2ch, miss next 2 ch, 1tr in next ch] to end, turn – 13 chsps.

2nd row: 5ch (counts as 1tr and 2ch throughout), miss first chsp, 1tr in next tr, *2ch, miss next chsp, 1tr in next tr*; repeat from * to * 4 times more, 2tr in next chsp, 1tr in next tr, repeat from * to * 5 times, 2ch, miss next 2 ch, 1tr in next ch, turn.

3rd row: 5ch, miss first chsp, 1tr in next tr, *2ch, miss next chsp, 1tr in next tr*; repeat from * to * 4 times more, 1tr in each of next 3 tr, repeat from * to * 5 times, 2ch, miss next 2 ch, 1tr in next ch, turn.

4th row: 5ch, miss first chsp, 1tr in next tr, *2ch, miss next chsp, 1tr in next tr*; repeat from * to * twice more, [2tr in next chsp, 1tr in next tr] twice, 2ch, miss next 2 tr, 1tr in next tr, [2tr in next chsp, 1tr in next tr] twice, repeat from * to * 3 times, 2ch, miss 2 ch, 1tr in next ch, turn.

5th row: 5ch, miss first chsp, 1tr in next tr, *2ch, miss next chsp, 1tr in next tr*; repeat from * to * once more, 2tr in next chsp, 1tr in next tr, 2ch, miss next 2 tr, 1tr in each of next 4 tr, 5ch, miss next chsp, 1tr in each of next 4 tr, 2ch, miss next 2 tr, 1tr in next tr, 2tr in next chsp, 1tr in next tr, repeat from * to * twice, 2ch, miss next 2 ch, 1tr in next ch, turn.

6th row: 5ch, miss first chsp, 1tr in next tr, *2ch, miss next chsp, 1tr in next tr*; repeat from * to * once more, 1tr in each of next 3 tr, 2tr in next chsp, 1tr in next tr, 5ch, miss next 3 tr, 1dc in next chsp, 5ch, miss next 3 tr, 1tr in next tr, 2tr in next chsp, 1tr in each of next 4 tr, repeat from * to * twice, 2ch, miss next 2 ch, 1tr in next ch, turn.

7th row: 5ch, miss first chsp, 1tr in next tr, [2tr in next chsp, 1tr in next tr] twice, 2ch, miss next 2 tr, 1tr in next tr, 5ch, miss next 3 tr, [1dc in next chsp, 5ch] twice, miss next 3 tr, 1tr in next tr, 2ch, miss next 2 tr, 1tr in next tr, [2tr in next chsp, 1tr in next tr] twice, 2ch, miss next 2 ch, 1tr in next ch, turn.

8th row: 5ch, miss first chsp, 1tr in next tr, *2ch, miss next 2 tr, 1tr in next tr*; repeat from * to * once more, 2tr in next chsp, 1tr in next tr, 3tr in next chsp, 5ch, 1dc in next chsp, 5ch, 3tr in next chsp, 1tr in next tr, 2tr in next chsp, 1tr in next tr, repeat from * to * twice, 2ch, miss next 2 ch, 1tr in next ch, turn.

9th row: 5ch, miss first chsp, 1tr in next tr, *2ch, miss next chsp, 1tr in next tr*; repeat from * to * once more, 1tr in each of next 3 tr, 2ch, miss next 2 tr, 1tr in next tr, 3tr in next chsp, 2ch, 3tr in next chsp, 1tr in next tr, 2ch, miss next 2 tr, 1tr in each of next 4 tr, repeat from * to * twice, 2ch, miss next 2 ch, 1tr in next ch, turn.

10th row: 5ch, miss first chsp, 1tr in next tr, *2ch, miss next chsp, 1tr in next tr*; repeat from * to * once more, 2ch, miss next 2 tr, 1tr in next tr, 2tr in next chsp, 1tr in each of next 4 tr, 2ch, miss next chsp, 1tr in each of next 4 tr, 2tr in next chsp, 1tr in next tr, 2ch, miss next 2 tr, 1tr in next tr, repeat from * to * twice, 2ch, miss next 2 ch, 1tr in next ch, turn.

11th row: 5ch, miss first chsp, 1tr in next tr, *2ch, miss next chsp, 1tr in next tr*; repeat from * to * twice more, [2ch, miss next 2 tr, 1tr in next tr] twice, 2tr in next chsp, 1tr in next tr, [2ch, miss

PATTERN NOTES

• Yarn amounts are based on average requirements and are therefore approximate. Instructions in square brackets are worked as stated after 2nd bracket.

Create strips of crochet squares to make this delicate bed cover

next 2 tr, 1tr in next tr] twice, repeat from * to * 3 times, 2ch, miss next 2 ch, 1tr in next ch, turn.

12th row: As 3rd row.

13th row: 5ch, miss first chsp, 1tr in next tr, *2ch, miss next chsp, 1tr in next tr*; repeat from * to * 4 times more, 2ch, miss next 2 tr, 1tr in next tr, repeat from * to * 5 times, 2ch, miss next 2 ch, 1tr in next ch, do not turn. ***

Edging round: 8ch (counts as 1tr and 5ch), 4tr in first corner sp, *2ch, miss next sp, [4tr in next sp, 2ch, miss next sp] 5 times**, [4tr, 5ch, 4tr] all in next corner sp*; repeat from * to * twice more, then repeat from * to ** once more, 3tr in corner sp at beginning of round, slst in 3rd ch of beginning 8ch. Fasten off.

Second square: Work as given for first square to ***.

Joining round: With wrong sides together, matching pattern so the 13th rows are aligned and facing in the same direction and with second square in front of first square, join one side-edge of squares thus, 5ch (counts as 1tr and 2ch), slst in chsp at corner of first square, 2ch, 4tr in corner sp of second square, [1ch, slst in next chsp of first square, 1ch, miss next sp of second square and work 4tr in following sp] 6 times, 2ch, slst in chsp at corner of first square, 2ch, 4tr in same corner sp of second square, complete second square in the same way as given on edging round of first square, ending with 3tr in corner sp at beginning of round, slst in 3rd ch of beginning 5ch. Fasten off.

Make a further 8 squares and join them in the same way as the second square was joined to the first, thus making the first strip 10 squares wide.

SECOND STRIP

Eleventh square: Work as given for first square to ***.

Joining round: Work as edging round of first square to **, 4tr in next corner sp, 2ch, then with wrong sides together, having eleventh square in front of first square of first strip and with 13th row of squares at bottom, join these edges thus, slst in chsp at corner of first square, 2ch, 4tr in corner sp of eleventh square, [1ch, slst in next chsp of first square, 1ch, miss next sp of eleventh square and work 4tr in following sp] 6 times, 2ch, slst in corner join on first strip, 2ch, 4tr in same corner sp of eleventh square, complete eleventh square in the same way as given on edging round of first square, ending with: 3tr in corner sp at beginning of round, slst in 3rd ch of beginning 8ch. Fasten off.

Twelfth square: Work as given for first square to ***.

Joining round: With wrong sides together, 13th row aligned and twelfth square in front of eleventh square, join edges thus, 5ch (counts as 1tr and 2ch), slst in chsp at corner on eleventh square, 2ch, 4tr in corner sp on twelfth square, *[1ch, slst in next chsp on eleventh square, 1ch, miss next sp on eleventh square and work 4tr in following sp] 6 times, 2ch, slst in corner join, 2ch, 4tr in same corner sp on twelfth square*; repeat from * to * once, joining to second square of first strip, then complete

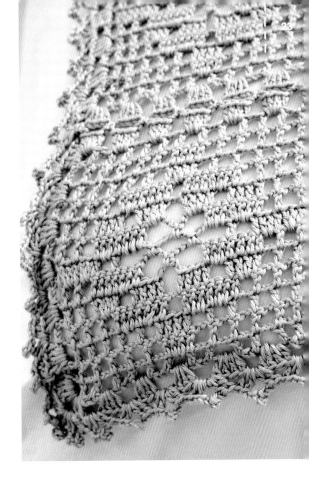

twelfth square in the same way as given on edging round of first square, ending with 3tr in corner sp at beginning of round, slst in 3rd ch of beginning 5ch. Fasten off. Make a further 8 squares and join them in the same way as the twelfth square was joined to the eleventh square and to the first strip.

THIRD TO TENTH STRIPS

Make and join a further 8 strips in the same way, thus making the bedspread 10 squares long and 10 squares wide.

EDGING

With right side facing, and with 3mm hook, join yarn to any corner chsp, 3ch (counts as 1tr), **work [1tr, [5ch, slst in 3rd ch from hook (a picot made here and throughout), 2ch, 2tr] 3 times] all in same corner chsp, [miss next 4 tr, work [2tr, 5ch, slst in 3rd ch from hook, 2ch, 2tr] all in next sp] 6 times, *work [2tr, 5ch, slst in 3rd ch from hook, 2ch, 2tr] all in next join, [miss next 4 tr, work [2tr, 5ch, slst in 3rd ch from hook, 2ch, 2tr] all in next sp] 6 times*; repeat from * to * to next corner chsp, work 1tr in corner chsp**, work from ** to ** 3 times more, omitting 1tr at end of last repeat, slst in 3rd ch of beginning 3ch.

Fasten off and neaten ends. Press according to ball band.

Crochet Card

Love is in the air in the form of lots of hearts! Spread the joy with thoughtful gifts for the special people in your life

DIFFICULTY

✕ ✕ ✕ ✕

WHAT YOU NEED

• 3.5mm crochet hook
• 40cm length of lace trimming
• Matching sewing thread

• 15cm square card with envelope
• Glue
• Rico Essentials Merino DK (100% wool)
  Colour: 1 x 50g (120m) Magenta (10)

MEASUREMENTS

Approx. 8cm/3in wide and 6cm/2¼in high.

ABBREVIATIONS

St(s), stitch(es); ch, chain; dc, double crochet; slst, slip stitch; chsp, chain space.

HEART MOTIF

Work with right side facing.

With 3.5mm hook, make 15ch.

1st round: 3dc in 2nd ch from hook, 1dc in each of next 5 ch, miss 2 ch, 1dc in each of next 5 ch, 3dc in last ch, work along other side of ch thus: 1dc in each of next 5 ch, (1dc, 2ch, 1dc) in chsp, 1dc in each of last 5 ch – 30 sts.

2nd round: 2dc in each of first 3 sts, 1dc in each of next 4 sts, miss next 2 sts, 1dc in each of next 4 sts, 2dc in each of next 3 sts, 1dc in each of next 6 sts, (1dc, 2ch, 1dc) in chsp, 1dc in each of last 6 sts – 36 sts.

3rd round: 2dc in next st, [1dc in next st, 2dc in next st] twice, 1dc in each of next 4 sts, miss next 2 sts, 1dc in each of next 4 sts, [2dc in next st, 1dc in next st] twice, 2dc in next st, 1dc in each of next 7 sts, (1dc, 2ch, 1dc) in chsp, 1dc in each of last 7 sts – 42 sts.

4th round: 1dc in next st, [2dc in next st, 1dc in each of next 2 sts] twice, 2dc in next st, 1dc in each of next 3 sts, miss next 2 sts, 1dc in each of next 3 sts, [2dc in next st, 1dc in each of next 2 sts] twice, 2dc in next st, 1dc in each of next 9 sts, work 1dc, 2ch and 1dc in chsp, 1dc in each of last 8 sts, slst in first dc – 48 sts. Fasten off. With sewing thread, work a running stitch around straight edge of lace trim and pull up so that this edge fits around outer edge of heart motif. Sew gathered edge of trim along top of last round on wrong side of overlapping ends at point. Position and glue motif to front of card.

PATTERN NOTES

• Yarn amounts are based on average
requirements and are therefore
approximate. Instructions in square
brackets are worked as stated after
2nd bracket.

*Its handy that the symbol for love can be formed so easily
with a motif made up of rounds of double crochet*

Happy Days

Want to add colour to a celebration?
Choose bright bunting!

PATTERN NOTES

- Yarn amounts are based on average requirements and are therefore approximate. Instructions in square brackets are worked as stated after 2nd bracket.

DIFFICULTY

✕ ✕ ✕ ✕

WHAT YOU NEED

• 4.00 crochet hook
• 2.5m of 1cm-wide ribbon
• 10 x 10cm square of stiff card.

• DMC Woolly (100% wool)
Colour 1: 1 x 50g (125m) Red (55)
Colour 2: 1 x 50g (125m) Yellow (93)
Colour 3: 1 x 50g (125m) Green (81)
Colour 4: 1 x 50g (125m) Turquoise (74)
Colour 5: 1 x 50g (125m) Orange (10)

MEASUREMENTS

Each pennant measures approximately
13.5cm/5¼in along each side.

ABBREVIATIONS

Ch, chain; st, stitch; tr, treble; dc, double crochet;
chsp, chain space; slst, slip st.

PENNANT (MAKE 9)

Use shades in a different order for each pennant.

1st round: With 4.00 hook and first shade, wind yarn round index
finger of left hand to form a slip ring, insert hook into ring, yarn
round hook and pull through, 3ch (counts as 1tr throughout), work
2tr in ring, 3ch, [3tr in ring, 3ch] twice, slst in top of 3ch and pull end
tightly to close ring.
Fasten off.

2nd round: Join in second shade to any chsp, 3ch, work 2tr, 3ch
and 3tr all in same place as join, 1tr in each of next
3tr, [work 3tr, 3ch and 3tr all in next chsp, 1tr in each of next 3tr]
twice, slst in top of 3ch.
Fasten off.

3rd round: Join in third shade to any chsp, 3ch, work 2tr, 3ch and 3tr
all in same place as join, 1tr in each of next
9tr, [work 3tr, 3ch and 3tr all in next chsp, 1tr in each of next 9tr]
twice, slst in top of 3ch.
Fasten off.

4th round: Join in fourth shade to any chsp, 3ch, work 2tr, 3ch and
3tr all in same place as join, 1tr in each of next 15tr, [work 3tr, 3ch
and 3tr all in next chsp, 1tr in each of next 15tr] twice, slst in top of
3ch. Fasten off.

Edging round: Join in fifth shade to any chsp, 1ch (does not count
as a st), 3dc in same place as join, 1dc in each of next 21tr, [3dc in
next chsp, 1dc in each of next 21tr] twice, slst in first dc.
Fasten off.

TO MAKE BUNTING

First make a tassel for each pennant in the same shade as last
round as follows: Wind yarn around centre of card thirty times. With
sharp scissors, cut yarn through all strands along one side edge of
card. Lay strands flat and tie them together securely around middle,
leaving ends of tie free to sew tassel to pennant. Fold strands in
half. To hold strands together, wrap a length of yarn around strands,
2.5cm down from fold and fasten off securely. Trim ends of tassel
to desired length.

Pin out pennants flat and even. Spray each triangle with cold water
and leave to dry. Spray each tassel, straighten strands and hang to
dry. When dry, sew a tassel to tip of each pennant. Thread ribbon
through corners at top edge of each pennant.

Granny Square Throw

Create this wonderfully colourful, shabby chic throw using a large motif in a mix of colours

PATTERN NOTES

• Yarn amounts are based on average requirements and are therefore approximate. Instructions in square brackets are worked as stated after 2nd bracket.

DIFFICULTY ✂ ✂ ✂ ✂

WHAT YOU NEED

• 4.00 crochet hook
• Of Bergere de France Ideal
  (40% wool, 30% acrylic, 30% polyamide)
  Key Colours:
  Colour 1: 3 x 50g (125m) Cream (51253)
  Colour 2: 3 x 50g (125m) Green (20754)
  Colour 3: 3 x 50g (125m) Fawn (23316)
  Colour 4: 2 x 50g (125m) Deep Pink (20555)
  Colour 5: 3 x 50g (125m) Pale Pink (23026)
  Other Colours:
  Colour 1: 2 x 50g (125m) Pale Blue (20933)
  Colour 2: 2 x 50g (125m) Dark Grey (54695)
  Colour 3: 2 x 50g (125m) Dusky Pink (35177)

Colour 4: 1 x 50g (125m) Mid Blue (20841)
Colour 5: 1 x 50g (125m) Pale Yellow (35166)
Colour 6: 1 x 50g (125m) Dark Green (25324)
Colour 7: 1 x 50g (125m) Purple (22375)
Colour 8: 1 x 50g (125m) Orange (24109)
Colour 9: 1 x 50g (125m) Pale Grey (24241)
Colour 10: 1 x 50g (125m) Light Teal (24257)
Colour 11: 1 x 50g (125m) Rust (35168)
Joining & Edging:
Colour: 25 x 50g (125m) White (51220)

MEASUREMENTS

The completed throw measures approximately
117 x 145cm/46 x 57in, including edging.

TENSION

Large motif measures approximately 24 x 24cm,
medium motif measures approximately 12 x 12cm
and small motif measures approximately 6 x 6cm;
using 4.00 hook

ABBREVIATIONS

Ch, chain; chsp, chain space; dc, double crochet;
htr, half treble; tr, treble; sp, space; st, stitch; slst, slip
stitch; yoh, yarn over hook; tr2tog, work 2tr together
thus: [yoh, insert hook in chsp, yoh and pull through,
yoh and pull through first 2 loops on hook] twice, yoh
and pull through all 3 loops on hook; tr3tog, work 3tr
together thus: [yoh, insert hook in chsp, yoh and pull
through, yoh and pull through first 2 loops on hook]
3 times, yoh and pull through all 4 loops on hook.

SQUARE ONE
LARGE MOTIF (MAKE 6)

Use 3 or more colours, varying the number of colours on each square
and include at least one of the key colours. Work all even-numbered
rounds in the same colour – colour Z.

1st round: With 4.00 hook and chosen colour, make 4ch, 2tr in 4th ch
from hook, 3ch, [3tr, 3ch] 3times in same place first 2tr, slst in 3rd of 3ch.
Fasten off.

2nd round: Join Z to any 3-chsp of last round, 1ch, [1dc, 3ch] twice in
same place as join, * [1dc, 3ch] twice in next 3-chsp, repeat from * twice
more, slst in first dc. Fasten off.

3rd round: Join next colour in last 3-chsp of last round, 3ch (counts as
1tr throughout), 2tr in same place as join, [work 3tr, 3ch and 3tr in corner
3-chsp, 3tr in next 3-chsp] 3 times, work 3tr, 3ch and 3tr in last corner
3-chsp, slst in 3rd of 3ch. Fasten off.

4th round: Join Z in sp between 3-tr group at end and 3ch at start of last
round,1ch, 1dc in same place as join, 3ch, 1dc in next sp between 3-tr
groups, 3ch, *[1dc, 3ch] twice in corner 3-chsp, [1dc in next sp between
3-tr groups, 3ch] twice, repeat from * twice more, [1dc, 3ch] twice in
corner 3-chsp, slst in first dc. Fasten off.

5th round: Join next colour in last 3-chsp of last round, 3ch, 2tr in same
place as join, [3tr in each 3-chsp to corner, work 3tr, 3ch and 3tr in
corner 3-chsp] 4 times, slst in 3rd of 3ch. Fasten off.

6th round: Join Z in sp between 3-tr group at end and 3ch at start of last
round, 1ch, 1dc in same place as join, 3ch, * [1dc in next sp between
3-tr groups, 3ch] to corner, [1dc, 3ch] twice in corner 3-chsp, repeat from
* 3 times, slst in first dc. Fasten off.

7th to 16th rounds: Repeat 5th and 6th rounds 5 times. Fasten off.

17th round: Join next colour in last 3-chsp of last round, 2ch, 2dc in
same place as join, [3dc in each 3-chsp to corner, work 3dc, 1ch and
3dc in corner 3-chsp] 4 times, slst in 2nd of 2ch. Fasten off.

Trebles, DCs and chain are worked here to create a neat new look

SQUARE TWO
MEDIUM MOTIF 1 (MAKE 15)

Each square uses 4 colours, A, B, C and D. Use at least one key colour in each square, and other colours randomly to create a fun effect.

1st round: With 4.00 hook and A, make 4ch, 15tr in 4th ch from hook, slst in 3rd of 3ch.

2nd round: 4ch (counts as 1tr and 1ch), [1tr in next tr, 1ch] 15 times, slst in 3rd of 4ch.

3rd round: 3ch (counts as 1tr throughout), 2tr in first chsp, [1tr next tr, 2tr in next chsp] 15 times, slst in 3rd of 3ch. Fasten off A.
Join B in same place as slst.

4th round: 1ch, 1dc in same st, [3ch, miss 2tr, 1dc in next tr, 10ch, miss 2tr, 1dc in next tr, 3ch, miss 2tr, 1dc in next tr, 5ch, miss 2tr, 1dc in next tr] 4 times, omitting final dc, slst in first dc.

5th round: Slst in 3-chsp, 1ch, 1dc in same chsp, work 5tr, 3ch and 5tr in 10-chsp, [1dc in 3-chsp, 7tr in 5-chsp, 1dc in 3-chsp, work 5tr, 3ch and 5tr in 10-chsp] 3 times, 1dc in 3-chsp, 7tr in 5-chsp, slst in first dc. Fasten off B.
Join C in same place as slst.

6th round: 8ch (counts as 1tr and 5ch), miss 5tr, [work 1dc, 3ch and 1dc in 3-chsp, 5ch, miss 5tr, 1tr in next dc, 3ch, miss 3tr, 1dc in next tr, 3ch, miss 3tr, 1tr in next dc, 5ch, miss 5tr] 3 times, work 1dc, 3ch and 1dc in 3-chsp, 5ch, miss 5tr, 1tr in next dc, 3ch, miss 3tr, 1dc in next tr, 3ch, miss last 3tr, slst in 3rd of 8ch.

7th round: 3ch, 4tr in 5-chsp, * work 3tr, 3ch and 3tr in 3-chsp, 5tr in 5-chsp, [3tr in next 3-chsp] twice, 5tr in 5-chsp, repeat from * twice more, work 3tr, 3ch and 3tr in 3-chsp, 5tr in 5-chsp, [3tr in next 3-chsp] twice, slst in 3rd

of 3ch. Fasten off C.
Join D in same place as slst.
8th round: 1ch, 1dc in same st, 1dc in each tr and 3dc in each corner 3-chsp, slst in first dc.
Fasten off.

DIFFICULTY ✂ ✂ ✂ ✂

WHAT YOU NEED

• 4.00 crochet hook

• Of Bergere de France Ideal
(40% wool, 30% acrylic, 30% polyamide)
Key Colours:
Colour 1: 3 x 50g (125m) Cream (51253)
Colour 2: 3 x 50g (125m) Green (20754)
Colour 3: 3 x 50g (125m) Fawn (23316)
Colour 4: 2 x 50g (125m) Deep Pink (20555)
Colour 5: 3 x 50g (125m) Pale Pink (23026)
Other Colours:
Colour 1: 2 x 50g (125m) Pale Blue (20933)
Colour 2: 2 x 50g (125m) Dark Grey (54695)
Colour 3: 2 x 50g (125m) Dusky Pink (35177)

Colour 4: 1 x 50g (125m) Mid Blue (20841)
Colour 5: 1 x 50g (125m) Pale Yellow (35166)
Colour 6: 1 x 50g (125m) Dark Green (25324)
Colour 7: 1 x 50g (125m) Purple (22375)
Colour 8: 1 x 50g (125m) Orange (24109)
Colour 9: 1 x 50g (125m) Pale Grey (24241)
Colour 10: 1 x 50g (125m) Light Teal (24257)
Colour 11: 1 x 50g (125m) Rust (35168)
Joining & Edging:
Colour: 25 x 50g (125m) White (51220)

MEASUREMENTS

The completed throw measures approximately
117 x 145cm/46 x 57in, including edging.

TENSION

Large motif measures approximately 24 x 24cm,
medium motif measures approximately 12 x 12cm
and small motif measures approximately 6 x 6cm;
using 4.00 hook

ABBREVIATIONS

Ch, chain; chsp, chain space; dc, double crochet;
htr, half treble; tr, treble; sp, space; st, stitch; slst, slip
stitch; yoh, yarn over hook; tr2tog, work 2tr together
thus: [yoh, insert hook in chsp, yoh and pull through,
yoh and pull through first 2 loops on hook] twice, yoh
and pull through all 3 loops on hook; tr3tog, work 3tr
together thus: [yoh, insert hook in chsp, yoh and pull
through, yoh and pull through first 2 loops on hook]
3 times, yoh and pull through all 4 loops on hook.

SQUARE THREE
MEDIUM MOTIF 2 (MAKE 16)

Work squares in 2, 3 or 4 colours, changing colour at the end of every round. On 3 or 4 colour squares, use colours in sequence. Use at least one key colour in each square, and other colours randomly.

1st round: With 4.00 hook and first colour, make 6ch, [3tr, 2ch] 3 times in 6th ch from hook, 2tr in same place as before, slst in 3rd of 5ch. Fasten off.
Join new colour in any 2-chsp.

2nd round: 7ch (counts as 1tr and 4ch), 2tr in same 2-chsp, [1tr in each of next 3tr, work 2tr, 4ch and 2tr in next 2-chsp] 3 times, 1tr in each of next 3tr, 1tr in same 2-chsp at base of 7ch, slst in 3rd of 7ch. Fasten off.
Join new colour in any 4-chsp.

3rd round: 1ch, [5dc in 4-chsp, 1dc in each of next 3tr, insert hook in next tr, yoh and pull loop through, insert hook in st in round below same tr, yoh and pull loop through, yoh and pull through all 3 loops – spike st made, 1dc in each of next 3tr] 4 times, slst in first dc.
Fasten off.
Join new colour in same place as slst.

4th round: 3ch (counts as 1tr throughout), 1tr in next dc, [4ch, miss next dc, 1tr in each of next 11 sts] 3 times, 4ch, miss next dc, 1tr in each of last 9 sts, slst in 3rd of 3ch. Fasten off.
Join new colour in same place as slst.

5th round: 3ch, 1tr in next tr, [work 2tr, 4ch and 2tr in 4-chsp, 1tr in each of next 11 sts] 3 times, work 2tr, 4ch and 2tr in 4-chsp, 1tr in each of last 9 sts, slst in 3rd of 3ch. Fasten off.
Join new colour in same place as slst.

6th round: 1ch, 1dc in same st, 1dc in each of next 3tr, [5dc in 4-chsp, 1dc in each of next 4tr, spike st in next tr, 1dc in each of next 5tr, spike st in next tr, 1dc in each of next 4 sts] 3 times, 5dc in 4-chsp, 1dc in each of next 4tr, spike st in next tr, 1dc in each of next 5tr, spike st in last tr,

slst in first dc. Fasten off.
Join new colour in same place as slst.

7th round: 3ch, 1tr in each of next 5dc, [4ch, miss 1dc, 1tr in each of next 19 sts] 3 times, 4ch, miss 1dc, 1tr in each of last 13 sts, slst in 3rd of 3ch. Fasten off.
Join new colour in same place as slst.

8th round: 3ch, 1tr in each of next 5tr, [work 2tr, 4ch and 2tr in 4-chsp, 1tr in each of next 19tr] 3 times, work 2tr, 4ch and 2tr in 4-chsp, 1tr in each of last 13tr, slst in 3rd of 3ch.
Fasten off.

SQUARE FOUR
MEDIUM MOTIF 3 (MAKE 28)

Each square uses 4 colours, A, B, C and D. Use at least one of the
key colours in each square, and other colours randomly.

1st round: With 4.00 hook and A, make 4ch, 1tr in 4th ch from hook,
3ch, slst into 3rd ch from hook – picot worked, [3tr, picot] 7 times in
same place as first tr, 1tr in same place as first tr, slst in top of first
3ch. Fasten off A.

Join B to centre tr of any 3-tr group.

2nd round: 1ch, 1dc in same st, 6ch, [1dc in centre tr of next 3-tr
group, 6ch] 7 times, slst in first dc.

3rd round: 1ch, [work 3dc, 3ch, 1dc, 3ch and 3dc all in next 6-chsp,
9ch, work 3dc, 3ch, 1dc, 3ch and 3dc all in next 6-chsp] 4 times, slst
to first dc. Fasten off B.

Join C to centre of any 9-chsp.

4th round: 1ch, [3dc in 9-chsp, 4ch, miss next 3-chsp, 1dc in next
3-chsp, 4ch, 1dc in next 3-chsp, 4ch, miss next 3-chsp] 4 times, slst
in first dc.

5th round: 3ch (counts as 1tr), * work 1tr, 1ch, 1tr, 1ch and 1tr all in next
dc, [1tr in next dc, 4tr in 4-chsp] 3 times, 1tr in next dc, repeat from *
3 times more, omitting 1tr at end of final repeat, slst in 3rd of 3ch.

6th round: 3ch, 1tr in next tr, [1tr in 1-chsp, work 1tr, 1ch, 1tr, 1ch and
1tr all in next tr, 1tr in 1-chsp, 1tr in each of next 18tr] 3 times, 1tr in
1-chsp, work 1tr, 1ch, 1tr, 1ch and 1tr all in next tr, 1tr in next chsp,
1tr in each of last 16tr, slst in 3rd of 3ch. Fasten off C.

Join D to same st as slst.

7th round: 1ch, 1dc in same st as join, 1dc in each of next 3tr, [1dc
in 1-chsp, 3dc in next tr, 1dc in 1-chsp, 1dc in each of next 22tr]
3 times, 1dc in 1-chsp, 3dc in next tr, 1dc in 1-chsp, 1dc in each of
last 18tr, slst in first dc.

Fasten off.

DIFFICULTY ✕ ✕ ✕ ✕

WHAT YOU NEED
• 4.00 crochet hook
• Of Bergere de France Ideal
  (40% wool, 30% acrylic, 30% polyamide)
  Key Colours:
  Colour 1: 3 x 50g (125m) Cream (51253)
  Colour 2: 3 x 50g (125m) Green (20754)
  Colour 3: 3 x 50g (125m) Fawn (23316)
  Colour 4: 2 x 50g (125m) Deep Pink (20555)
  Colour 5: 3 x 50g (125m) Pale Pink (23026)
  Other Colours:
  Colour 1: 2 x 50g (125m) Pale Blue (20933)
  Colour 2: 2 x 50g (125m) Dark Grey (54695)
  Colour 3: 2 x 50g (125m) Dusky Pink (35177)

Colour 4: 1 x 50g (125m) Mid Blue (20841)
Colour 5: 1 x 50g (125m) Pale Yellow (35166)
Colour 6: 1 x 50g (125m) Dark Green (25324)
Colour 7: 1 x 50g (125m) Purple (22375)
Colour 8: 1 x 50g (125m) Orange (24109)
Colour 9: 1 x 50g (125m) Pale Grey (24241)
Colour 10: 1 x 50g (125m) Light Teal (24257)
Colour 11: 1 x 50g (125m) Rust (35168)
Joining & Edging:
Colour: 25 x 50g (125m) White (51220)

MEASUREMENTS

The completed throw measures approximately
117 x 145cm/46 x 57in, including edging.

TENSION

Large motif measures approximately 24 x 24cm,
medium motif measures approximately 12 x 12cm
and small motif measures approximately 6 x 6cm;
using 4.00 hook

ABBREVIATIONS

Ch, chain; chsp, chain space; dc, double crochet;
htr, half treble; tr, treble; sp, space; st, stitch; slst, slip
stitch; yoh, yarn over hook; tr2tog, work 2tr together
thus: [yoh, insert hook in chsp, yoh and pull through,
yoh and pull through first 2 loops on hook] twice, yoh
and pull through all 3 loops on hook; tr3tog, work 3tr
together thus: [yoh, insert hook in chsp, yoh and pull
through, yoh and pull through first 2 loops on hook]
3 times, yoh and pull through all 4 loops on hook.

SQUARES FIVE & SIX
SMALL MOTIF 1 (MAKE 54)

Each square uses 3 colours, A, B and C. Use at least one key colour in
each square, and other colours randomly.

1st round: With 4.00 hook and A, make 4ch, 15tr in 4th ch from hook,
slst in 3rd of 3ch – 16 sts.

2nd round: 2ch (counts as 1htr), 1htr next st, work 2tr, 2ch and 2tr all
in next st, [1htr in each of next 3 sts, work 2tr, 2ch and 2tr all in next st]
3 times, 1htr in last st, slst in 2nd of 2ch.
Fasten off A.

Join B in same place as slst.

3rd round: 4ch (counts as 1tr and 1ch), miss next st, 1tr in next st, 1ch,
miss next st, * work 2tr, 2ch and 2tr all in next 2-chsp, [1ch, miss next st,
1tr in next st] 3 times, 1ch, miss next st, repeat from * twice more, work
2tr, 2ch and 2tr all in last 2-chsp, 1ch, miss next st, 1tr in next st, 1ch,
miss last st, slst in 3rd of 4ch.
Fasten off B.

Join C in same place as slst.

4th round: 1ch, 1dc into each tr and chsp, working 1dc, 1ch and 1dc all
in each corner 2-chsp, slst in first dc. Fasten off.

SMALL MOTIF 2 (MAKE 10)

Each square uses 3 colours, A, B and C. Use at least one key colour in
each square, and other colours randomly to create a unique effect.

1st round: With 4.00 hook and A, make 4ch, 23tr in 4th ch from hook,
slst in 3rd of 3ch – 24 sts.

2nd round: 6ch (counts as 1dc and 5ch), miss next 2tr, [1dc in next tr,
5ch, miss next 2tr] 7 times, slst in first of 6ch.
Fasten off A.

Join B in any 5-chsp.

3rd round: 3ch, tr2tog in 5-chsp, 3ch, [tr3tog, 3ch] twice in same 5-chsp,

1dc in next 5-chsp, 3ch, * [tr3tog, 3ch] 3 times in next 5-chsp, 1dc in next
5-chsp, 3ch, repeat from * twice more, slst in top of tr2tof. Fasten off B.
Join C in same place as slst.

4th round: 1ch, 1dc in tr2tog, [2dc in next 3-chsp, 1dc, 1ch and 1dc all
in next tr3tog, 2dc in next 3-chsp, 1dc in next tr3tog, 2dc in next 3-chsp,
1dc in next dc, 2dc in next 3-chsp, 1dc in next tr3tog] 4 times, omitting
final dc, slst in first dc. Fasten off.

DIFFICULTY ✕ ✕ ✕ ✕

WHAT YOU NEED

- 4.00 crochet hook
- Of Bergere de France Ideal
  (40% wool, 30% acrylic, 30% polyamide)

KEY COLOURS:

Colour 1: 3 x 50g (125m) Cream (51253)
Colour 2: 3 x 50g (125m) Green (20754)
Colour 3: 3 x 50g (125m) Fawn (23316)
Colour 4: 2 x 50g (125m) Deep Pink (20555)
Colour 5: 3 x 50g (125m) Pale Pink (23026)

OTHER COLOURS:

Colour 1: 2 x 50g (125m) Pale Blue (20933)
Colour 2: 2 x 50g (125m) Dark Grey (54695)
Colour 3: 2 x 50g (125m) Dusky Pink (35177)

Colour 4: 1 x 50g (125m) Mid Blue (20841)
Colour 5: 1 x 50g (125m) Pale Yellow (35166)
Colour 6: 1 x 50g (125m) Dark Green (25324)
Colour 7: 1 x 50g (125m) Purple (22375)
Colour 8: 1 x 50g (125m) Orange (24109)
Colour 9: 1 x 50g (125m) Pale Grey (24241)
Colour 10: 1 x 50g (125m) Light Teal (24257)
Colour 11: 1 x 50g (125m) Rust (35168)

Joining & Edging:

Colour: 25 x 50g (125m) White (51220)

MEASUREMENTS

The completed throw measures approximately
117 x 145cm/46 x 57in, including edging.

TENSION

Large motif measures approximately 24 x 24cm,
medium motif measures approximately 12 x 12cm
and small motif measures approximately 6 x 6cm;
using 4.00 hook

ABBREVIATIONS

Ch, chain; chsp, chain space; dc, double crochet;
htr, half treble; tr, treble; sp, space; st, stitch; slst, slip
stitch; yoh, yarn over hook; tr2tog, work 2tr together
thus: [yoh, insert hook in chsp, yoh and pull through,
yoh and pull through first 2 loops on hook] twice,
yoh and pull through all 3 loops on hook; tr3tog,
work 3tr together thus: [yoh, insert hook in chsp,
yoh and pull through, yoh and pull through first 2
loops on hook] 3 times, yoh and pull through all 4
loops on hook.

PUT IT TOGETHER
TO MAKE UP

Follow the diagram below for positioning of
squares to create a fun, jumbled look.

TO JOIN SMALL SQUARES

With wrong sides together, join Everest to
corner, 1ch, join with dc in back loop only of
each st to corner. Fasten off.

TO JOIN MEDIUM AND LARGE SQUARES

With wrong sides together, join Everest to
corner of first square, 2ch, 1htr in corner of
second square, [1ch, miss 1 st on first square
and work 1htr in next st, 1ch, miss 1 st on
second square and work 1htr in next st] to
next corner, noting that sts may not match up
equally and to even squares out, it may be
necessary to miss an extra st occasionally.
Fasten off.

EDGING

With right side facing, join Everest to one
corner of throw, 1ch, 1dc in corner, [miss 2 sts,
5tr in next st, miss 2 sts, 1dc in next st] around
outer edge, omitting 1dc at end, slst in first dc.
Fasten off.

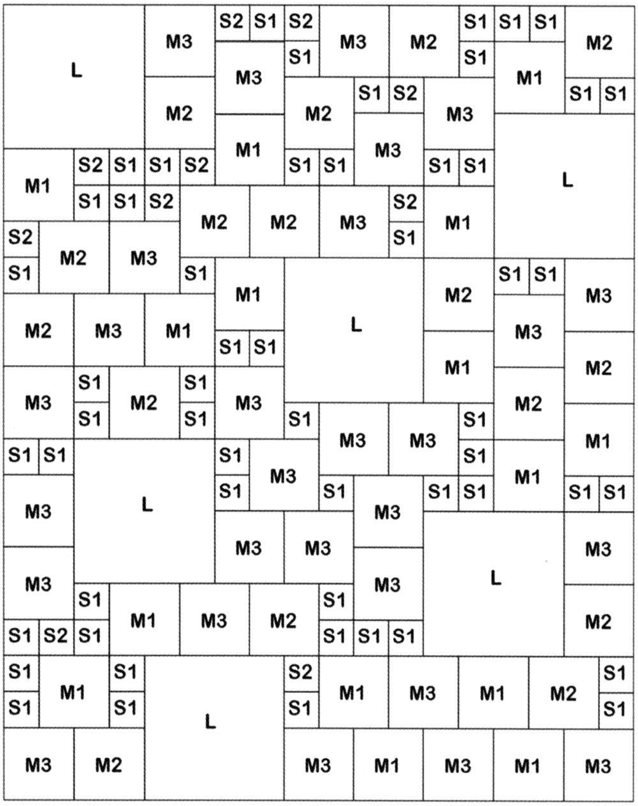

KEY   L – large motif   M2 – medium motif 2   S1 – small motif 1
          M1 – medium motif 1   M3 – medium motif 3   S2 – small motif 2

Hanging Plant Pot Holders

Brighten up any space with these handy pot holders for your indoor plants

DIFFICULTY

✕ ✕ ✕ ✕

WHAT YOU NEED

• 6.00 crochet hook
• one large and one small plant pot in sizes given in measurements
• Wendy Supreme Luxury Cotton Chunky (100% cotton)

Large plant pot holder:
Colour: 1 x 100g (83m) Peacock (35)
Small plant pot holder:
Colour: 1 x 100g (83m) Cerise (33)

MEASUREMENTS
Large plant pot holder:
To fit a plant pot approx 11cm/4¼in diameter at base, 15cm/6in diameter at top edge and

13cm/5in tall.
Small plant pot holder:
To fit a plant pot approx 9cm/3½in diameter at base, 11cm/4¼in diameter at top edge and 9.5cm/3¾in tall.

ABBREVIATIONS
Ch, chain; st, stitch; dc, double crochet; tr, treble; slst, slip st; chsp, chain space.

LARGE PLANT POT HOLDER

1st round: With 6.00 hook and Peacock, wind yarn round index finger of left hand to form a ring, insert hook into ring, yarn over hook and pull through, 4ch (counts as 1tr and 1ch), work [1tr in ring, 1ch] 9 times, slst in 3rd of 4ch, pull end tightly to close ring – 10chsp.

2nd round: Slst in first chsp, 3ch (counts as 1tr throughout), 1tr in same place as slst, 2ch, [2tr in next chsp, 2ch] 9 times, slst in top of 3ch – ten 2tr groups.

3rd round: 3ch, 1tr in next tr, 2tr in first chsp, [1tr in each of next 2tr, 2tr in next chsp] 9 times, slst in top of 3ch – 40tr.

4th round: 3ch, 2tr in base of 3ch, miss next tr, 1dc in next tr, miss next tr, [3tr in next tr, miss next tr, 1dc in next tr, miss next tr] 9 times, slst in top of 3ch.

5th round: Slst in next tr, 1ch (does not count as a st), 1dc in same place as slst, 3ch, [1dc in centre tr of next 3tr group, 3ch] 9 times, slst in first dc.

6th round: 3ch, 2tr in base of 3ch, 1dc in next chsp, [3tr in next dc, 1dc in next chsp] 9 times, slst in top of 3ch.

7th round: Slst in next tr, 1ch (does not count as a st), 1dc in same place as slst, 4ch, [1dc in centre tr of next 3tr group, 4ch] 9 times, slst in first dc.

8th round: 3ch, 2tr in base of 3ch, 1ch, 1dc in next chsp, 1ch, [3tr in next dc, 1ch, 1dc in next chsp, 1ch] 9 times, slst in top of 3ch.

9th and 10th rounds: As 7th and 8th rounds. Fasten off.

HANGING STRINGS

Cut 5 x 100cm lengths of Peacock and fold each length in half.

[With wrong side facing, insert 6.00 hook in centre tr of one 3tr group, place folded edge of one length over hook and pull loop through, take both strands over hook and pull through loop on hook, tighten and leave till later, miss next 3tr-group] 5 times.

Place pot in holder and make sure that strings are of equal lengths. Using photo as guide, knot strings together leaving ends free. Plait ends for approximately 6cm, knot ends together and trim.

PATTERN NOTES

• Yarn amounts are based on average requirements and are therefore approximate. Instructions in square brackets are worked as stated after 2nd bracket.

SMALL PLANT POT HOLDER

1st round: With 6.00 hook and Cerise, wind yarn round index finwger of left hand to form a ring, insert hook into ring, yarn over hook and pull through, 4ch (counts as 1tr and 1ch), work [1tr in ring, 1ch] 9 times, slst in 3rd of 4ch, pull end tightly to close ring – 10chsp.

2nd round: Slst in first chsp, 3ch (counts as 1tr throughout), 1tr in same place as slst, 2ch, [2tr in next chsp, 2ch] 9 times, slst in top of 3ch – ten 2tr groups.

3rd round: 1ch (does not count as a st throughout), 1dc in base of ch, 2dc in next tr, 1dc in next chsp, [1dc in each of next 2tr, 1dc in next chsp] 4 times, 1dc in next tr, 2dc in next tr, 1dc in next chsp, [1dc in each of next 2tr, 1dc in next chsp] 4 times, slst in first dc.

4th round: 3ch, 2tr in base of 3ch, miss next dc, 1dc in next dc, miss next dc, [3tr in next dc, miss next dc, 1dc in next dc, miss next dc] 7 times, slst in top of 3ch – 8tr groups.

5th round: Slst in next tr, 1ch, 1dc in same place as slst, 3ch, [1dc in centre tr of next 3tr group, 3ch] 7 times, slst in first dc.

6th round: 3ch, 2tr in base of 3ch, 1ch, 1dc in next chsp, 1ch, [3tr in next dc, 1ch, 1dc in next chsp, 1ch] 7 times, slst in top of 3ch.

7th round: Slst in next tr, 1ch, 1dc in same place as slst, 4ch, [1dc in centre tr of next 3tr group, 4ch] 7 times, slst in first dc.

8th round: 3ch, 2tr in base of 3ch, 1ch, 1dc in next chsp, 1ch, [3tr in next dc, 1ch, 1dc in next chsp, 1ch] 7 times, slst in top of 3ch. Fasten off.

HANGING STRINGS

Cut 4 x 100cm lengths of Fuchsia and fold each length in half. [With wrong side facing, insert 6.00 hook in centre tr of one 3tr group, place folded edge of one length over hook and pull loop through, take both strands over hook and pull through loop on hook, tighten and leave till later, miss next 3tr-group] 4 times.

Place pot in holder and make sure that strings are of equal lengths. Using photo as guide, knot strings together leaving ends free. Plait ends for approximately 4cm, knot ends together and trim.

Hot Stuff

Pop our vintage-style cover on your hot-water bottle and cuddle up

DIFFICULTY

✕ ✕ ✕ ✕

WHAT YOU NEED

- 4.00 crochet hook
- DMC Woolly 5 (100% wool)
- Colour 1: 1 x 50g (80m) Mustard (10)

Colour 2: 1 x 50g (80m) Aqua (73)
Colour 3: 1 x 50g (80m) Green (89)
Colour 4: 1 x 50g (80m) Pale Blue (71)

MEASUREMENTS

Approximately 30.5 x 20.5cm/
12 x 8in excluding picot edging.

TENSION

1 motif measures 10 x 10cm, using 4.00 hook.

ABBREVIATIONS

Ch, chain; dc, double crochet; st, stitch; tr, treble; chsp, chain space; slst, slip stitch; sp, space.

FRONT

First motif: With 4.00 hook and Mustard, make 4ch, slst in first ch to form ring.

1st round: 3ch (counts as 1tr throughout), 2tr in ring, [2ch, 3tr in ring] 3 times, 2ch, slst in top of 3ch. Fasten off.
Join Aqua with slst to any chsp.

2nd round: 3ch, work 2tr, 2ch and 3tr all in same chsp as slst, [work 3tr, 2ch and 3tr all in next chsp] 3 times, slst in top of 3ch. Fasten off.
Join Green with slst to any chsp.

3rd round: 3ch, work 2tr, 3ch and 3tr all in same chsp as slst, [3tr in sp after next 3tr group, work 3tr, 2ch and 3tr all in next chsp] 3 times, 3tr in sp after next 3tr group, slst in top of 3ch.
Fasten off.
Join Pale Blue with slst to any chsp.

4th round: 3ch, work 2tr, 2ch and 3tr all in same chsp as slst, * [1ch, 3tr in sp after next 3tr group] twice, 1ch, work 3tr, 2ch and 3tr all in next chsp, repeat from * twice more, [1ch, 3tr in sp after next 3tr group] twice, 1ch, slst in top of 3ch. Fasten off.
Work another 5 motif, using colours as follows:
Second motif: Green, Pale Blue, Aqua and Mustard.
Third motif: Pale Blue, Mustard, Aqua and Green.
Fourth motif: Aqua, Mustard, Green and Pale Blue.
Fifth motif: Aqua, Pale Blue, Green and Mustard.
Sixth motif: Mustard, Aqua, Pale Blue and Green.
To complete front: Arrange motifs in 3 rows of 2 motifs each.
Join motifs horizontally as follows: With wrong sides of pair of motifs together and using 4.00 hook, join Aqua to back loop of ch at corner of both motifs, 1ch (does not counts as a st), inserting hook in back loop of each st on both motifs, work 1dc in each st to next corner, then continue in same way along next pair of motifs. Fasten off.

Work 1 more horizontal join across next two pairs of motifs. Fasten off.
Now, join motifs vertically in same way.
Edging: With right side facing and using 4.00 hook, join Aqua with slst to top right corner chsp, 1ch (does not count as a st), 3dc in same chsp as slst, * [1dc in each of next 3tr, 1dc in next chsp] 3 times, 1dc in each of next 3tr **, 1dc in next chsp, 1dc in seam, 1dc in chsp of next motif, work from * to **, 3dc in corner chsp, [work from * to **, 1dc in next chsp, 1dc in seam, 1dc in next chsp of next motif] twice, work from * to **, 3dc in corner chsp, repeat from * omitting last 3dc, slst in top of first dc – 180 sts. Fasten off.

BACK

Work as first motif on front using colours as follows:
First motif: Mustard, Aqua, Pale Blue and Green.
Second motif: Aqua, Pale Blue, Green and Mustard.
Third motif: Aqua, Mustard, Green and Pale Blue.
Fourth motif: Pale Blue, Mustard, Aqua and Green.
Fifth motif: Green, Pale Blue, Aqua and Mustard.
Sixth motif: Mustard, Aqua, Green and Pale Blue.
Complete back and work edging as on front.

PICOT EDGING

With wrong sides of both pieces together and front facing, using 4.00 hook, join Pale Blue with slst to back loop of 4th st before centre of 3dc at top left corner of shorter edge of both pieces, 1ch (does not count as a st), working in back loops of both motifs throughout, work 1dc in same st as slst, 3ch, slst in 3rd of 3ch – picot made, 1dc in each of next 4 sts around 3 sides, ending in centre 3dc at top right corner, 3ch, slst in 3rd of 3ch, 1dc each of next 4 sts, 3ch, slst in 3rd of 3ch, now work in back loop of each st along front edge only, [1dc in each of next 4dc, 3ch, slst in 3rd ch from hook] 6 times, 1dc in each of last 3dc, slst in first dc. Fasten off.

PATTERN NOTES

• Yarn amounts are based on average requirements and are therefore approximate. Instructions in square brackets are worked as stated after 2nd bracket.

PATTERN NOTES

- Yarn amounts are based on average requirements and are therefore approximate. Instructions in square brackets are worked as stated after 2nd bracket.

Double Quick

Two simple makes from a single ball of raffia. Genius!

DIFFICULTY

✕ ✕ ✕ ✕

WHAT YOU NEED

· 6.00 crochet hook

· Glass jar approximately 16.5cm/6 ⅛in high and 30.5cm/12in circumference

· King Cole Raffia (100% cellulose rayon)

Colour: 1 x 50g (114m) Natural (1456)

MEASUREMENTS

Jar cover:

Approximately 15cm/6in high and 9cm/3½in diameter.

Place mat:

Approximately 28cm/11in diameter.

ABBREVIATIONS

Ch, chain; dc, double crochet; tr, treble; slst, slip stitch; dtr, double treble; chsp, chain space.

SPIRAL CUSHION

First With 6.00 hook, make 6ch, slst in first ch to form a ring.

1st round: 4ch (counts as 1tr and 1ch), [1tr in ring, 1ch] 11 times, slst in 3rd of 4ch – 12 chsp.

2nd round: [2dc in next chsp] to end, slst in first dc – 24dc.

3rd round: 3ch (counts as 1tr), [2tr in next dc, 1tr in next dc] 11 times, 2tr in last dc, slst in top of 3ch – 36tr.

4th round: 1ch (counts as 1dc), [1dc in next tr] to end, slst in 1ch – 36dc.

5th round: 3ch (counts as 1tr), 1tr in base of 3ch, [miss next dc, 1dc in next dc, miss next dc, 3tr in next dc – a shell made] 8 times, miss next dc, 1dc in next dc, miss last dc, 1tr in base of 3ch, slst in top of 3ch – 9 shells.

6th round: [5ch, slst in centre tr of next shell] 8 times, 5ch, slst in base of 5ch at beginning.

7th round: 1ch, 3dc in next chsp, [1ch, 3dc in next chsp] 8 times, slst in 1ch.

8th round: 4ch (counts as 1tr and 1ch), 1tr in base of 4ch, [miss next dc, 1tr in next dc, miss next dc, work 1tr, 1ch and 1tr all in next chsp] 8 times, miss next dc, 1tr in next dc, miss last dc, slst in 3rd of 4ch.

9th round: Slst in next chsp, 3ch (counts as 1tr), 1tr in same chsp as slst, [miss next tr, 1dc in next tr, miss next tr, 3tr in next chsp] 8 times, miss next tr, 1dc in last tr, 1tr in same chsp as 3ch at beginning, slst in top of 3ch – 9 shells.

10th to 13th rounds: Work 6th to 9th rounds. Fasten off.

TO COMPLETE

Cut 65cm length of raffia and thread end evenly through stitches of last round, bringing ends out to tie in a bow.

PLACE MAT

1st to 3rd rounds: Work 1st to 3rd rounds of jar cover.

4th round: 1ch (counts as 1dc), 1dc in base of 1ch, [1dc in each of next 2tr, 2dc in next tr] 11 times, 1dc in each of last 2tr, slst in 1ch – 48dc.

5th round: 3ch (counts as 1tr), 2tr in base of 3ch, [miss next dc, slst in next dc, miss next dc, 5tr in next dc – a shell made] 11 times, miss next dc, slst in next dc, miss last dc, 2tr in base of 3ch, slst in top of 3ch – 12 shells.

6th round: 6ch (counts as 1dc and 5ch), [1dc in centre of next shell, 5ch] 11 times, slst in first of 6ch.

7th round: 3ch, [work 1tr, 2ch, 1tr, 2ch and 1tr all in next chsp, 1tr in next dc] 11 times, work 1tr, 2ch, 1tr, 2ch and 1tr all in last chsp, slst in top of 3ch.

8th round: [Miss next tr, 3tr into next chsp, 1ch, 1dtr in next tr, 1ch, 3tr in next chsp, miss next tr, slst in next tr] 12 times, ending last repeat with slst in same place as slst at end of last round.

Edging round: 1ch, [1dc in each of next 3tr, 1dc in next chsp, 3ch, 1dc in next chsp, 1dc in each of next 3tr, miss slst] 12 times, slst in first dc. Fasten off.

PATTERN NOTES

· Yarn amounts are based on average requirements and are therefore approximate. Instructions in square brackets are worked as stated after 2nd bracket.

Bobble Bag

This cute bag makes a great storage solution, especially for children's toys

DIFFICULTY

✂ ✂ ✂ ✂

WHAT YOU NEED

• 4.5 (No. 7) crochet hook
• Stylecraft Jeanie Denim Look
  (60% cotton, 40% acrylic)

Colour: 2 x 100g (210m) Dixie (9349)

MEASUREMENTS

Approximately 22cm/8¾in diameter and 16cm/6¼in high.

ABBREVIATIONS

Ch, chain; dc, double crochet; st, stitch; tr, treble; slst, slip st; chsp, chain space; yrh, yarn round hook; mb, make bobble (yrh, insert hook in next st, yrh and pull through, yrh and pull through first 2 loops on hook, [yrh, insert hook in same st, yrh and pull through, yrh and pull through first 2 loops on hook] 4 times, yrh and pull through all 6 loops on hook).

TO MAKE

Base: 1st round: With 4.5mm hook, wind yarn round index finger of left hand to form a slip ring, insert hook into ring, yarn over hook and pull through, 3ch (counts as 1tr throughout), work 1tr, [2ch, 2tr] 5 times into the ring, 2ch, slst in top of 3ch, pull end of yarn tightly to close ring – 12tr.

2nd round: 3ch, 1tr in next st, [work 1tr, 2ch and 1tr all in next chsp, 1tr in each of next 2 sts] 5 times, work 1tr, 2ch and 1tr all in last chsp, slst in top of 3ch – 24tr.

3rd round: 3ch, 1tr in each of next 2 sts, [work 1tr, 2ch and 1tr all in next chsp, 1tr in each of next 4 sts] 5 times, work 1tr, 2ch and 1tr all in last chsp, 1tr in last st, slst in top of 3ch – 36tr.

4th round: 3ch, 1tr in each of next 3 sts, [work 1tr, 2ch and 1tr all into next chsp, 1tr in each of next 6 sts] 5 times, work 1tr, 2ch and 1tr all in last chsp, 1tr in each of last 2 sts, slst in top of 3ch – 48tr.

5th round: 3ch, 1tr in each of next 4 sts, [work 1tr, 2ch and 1tr all in next chsp, 1tr in each of next 8 sts] 5 times, work 1tr, 2ch and 1tr all in last chsp, 1tr in each of last 3 sts, slst in top of 3ch – 60tr.

6th round: 3ch, 1tr in each of next 5 sts, [work 1tr, 2ch and 1tr all in next chsp, 1tr in each of next 10 sts] 5 times, work 1tr, 2ch and 1tr all in last chsp, 1tr in each of last 4 sts, slst in top of 3ch – 72tr.

7th round: 3ch, 1tr in each of next 6 sts, [work 1tr, 2ch and 1tr all in next chsp, 1tr in each of next 12 sts] 5 times, work 1tr, 2ch and 1tr all in last chsp, 1tr in each of last 5 sts, slst in top of 3ch – 84tr.

8th round: 3ch, 1tr in each of next 7 sts, [work 1tr, 2ch and 1tr all in last chsp, 1tr in each of last 6 sts, slst in top of 3ch – 96tr.

9th round: 3ch, 1tr in each of next 8 sts, [work 1tr, 2ch and 1tr all in next chsp, 1tr in each of next 16 sts] 5 times, work 1tr, 2ch and 1tr all in last chsp, 1tr in each of last 7 sts, slst in top of 3ch – 108tr.

10th round: 3ch, 1tr in each of next 9 sts, [work 1tr, 2ch and 1tr all in next chsp, 1tr in each of next 18 sts] 5 times, work 1tr, 2ch and 1tr all in next chsp, 1tr in each of last 8 sts, slst in top of 3ch – 120tr.

11th round: 3ch, 1tr in each of next 10 sts, [work 1tr, 2ch and 1tr all in next chsp, 1tr in each of next 20 sts] 5 times, work 1tr, 2ch and 1tr all in last chsp, 1tr in each of last 9 sts, slst in top of 3ch – 132tr.

12th round: 3ch, 1tr in each of next 11 sts, [work 1tr, 2ch and 1tr all in next chsp, 1tr in each of next 22 sts] 5 times, work 1tr, 2ch and 1tr all in last chsp, 1tr in each of last 10 sts, slst in top of 3ch – 144tr.

13th round: 3ch, 1tr in each of next 12 sts, [2tr in next chsp, 1tr in each of next 24 sts] 5 times, 2tr in last chsp, 1tr in each of last 11 sts, slst in top of 3ch – 156dc.

Sides: 14th round: 3ch, [mb in next st, 1tr in each of next 5 sts] to last 5 sts, mb in next st, 1tr in each of last 4 sts, slst in top of 3ch.

15th round: 3ch, [1tr in next st] to end.

16th round: 3ch, 1tr in each of next 3 sts, [mb in next st, 1tr in each of next 5 sts] to last 2 sts, mb in next st, 1tr in last st, slst in top of 3ch.

17th round: As 15th round. Repeat 14th to 17th rounds, 3 times more, then work 14th and 15th rounds again.

Last round: 1ch (counts as 1dc), [1dc into next st] to end, slst in 1ch. Fasten off.

Make a chain cord 1m long for drawstring and thread through last bobble round.

Amigurumi Hearts

Show some love with these sweet hearts, which can also be incorporated into bigger projects

DIFFICULTY

✕ ✕ ✕ ✕

WHAT YOU NEED

• 4.00 crochet hook
• Washable toy stuffing
• DMC Woolly (100% wool)

Colour 1: 1 x 50g (125m) Light Pink (042)
Colour 2: 1 x 50g (125m) Bright Orange (103)
Colour 3: 1 x 50g (125m) Mid Pink (043)
Colour 4: 1 x 50g (125m) Light Blue (073)
Colour 5: 1 x 50g (125m) Mid Green (077)
Colour 6: 1 x 50g (125m) Royal Blue (075)
Colour 7: 1 x 50g (125m) Lime Green (081)
Colour 8: 1 x 50g (125m) Mustard (091)

ABBREVIATIONS

Ch, chain; st, stitch; dc, double crochet; slst, slip st; dec, decrease; dc2tog, work 2dc together thus: [insert hook in next st, yarn round hook and pull through] twice, yarn round hook and pull through all 3 loops on hook.

TO MAKE

1st row: With 4.00 hook and chosen shade, make 2ch, work 3dc in 2nd ch from hook, turn.

2nd row: 1ch (does not count as a st), [2dc in next dc] 3 times, slst in first dc – 6dc.

Mark end of last round and move marker up at end of every round.

3rd round: [2dc in next dc, 1dc in next dc] 3 times – 9dc.

4th round: [2dc in next dc, 1dc in each of next 2dc] 3 times – 12dc.

5th round: [2dc in next dc, 1dc in each of next 3dc] 3 times – 15dc.

6th round: [2dc in next dc, 1dc in each of next 4dc] 3 times – 18dc.

7th round: [2dc in next dc, 1dc in each of next 5dc] 3 times – 21dc.

8th round: [2dc in next dc, 1dc in each of next 6dc] 3 times – 24dc.

Dividing round: [1dc in next dc] 12 times, miss next 12dc and bring yarn back to beginning of dividing round and work on these 12dc for first half.

First half: Next round: [1dc in next dc] 12 times.

1st dec round: [Dc2tog, 1dc in each of next 2dc] 3 times – 9dc.

2nd dec round: [Dc2tog, 1dc in next dc] 3 times – 6dc.

Break off yarn leaving a long end. Thread end through top of last round, pull up tightly and secure.

Stuff and continue to stuff as you go.

Second half: Rejoin yarn to end of dividing round and work [1dc in next dc] 12 times.

Bring yarn back to first of these 12 sts.

Next round: [1dc in next dc] 12 times.

1st dec round: [Dc2tog, 1dc in each of next 2dc] 3 times – 9dc.

2nd dec round: [Dc2tog, 1dc in next dc] 3 times – 6dc.

Break off yarn, leaving a long end. Thread end through top of last round, pull up tightly and secure.

TO COMPLETE

Close opening at beginning of heart.

Make 1 heart in each of the other 6 shades.

PATTERN NOTES

• Yarn amounts are based on average requirements and are therefore approximate. Instructions in square brackets are worked as stated after 2nd bracket.

PATTERN NOTES

· Yarn amounts are based on average
requirements and are therefore
approximate. Instructions in square
brackets are worked as stated after
2nd bracket.

Little Sweetheart

Button baby into a smart blue jacket, then wrap him up in a heart-scattered blanket. Perfectly cosy!

DIFFICULTY

✕ ✕ ✕ ✕

WHAT YOU NEED

· 3.00 & 3.50 crochet hooks
· Sirdar Cotton DK (100% cotton)
  Colour 1: 2 x 100g (212m) Bluebird (515)
  Colour 2: 1 x 100g (212m) Darling Bud (509)

Colour 3: 1 x 100g (212m) Lotus (532)
Colour 4: 1 x 100g (212m) Hot Pink (511)
Colour 5: 1 x 100g (212m) Sapling (529)
Colour 6: 1 x 100g (212m) Cool Aqua (519)

MEASUREMENTS

Approximately 50 x 50cm/19½ x 19½in.

TENSION

Each motif measures 10 x 10cm, using 3.50 hook.

ABBREVIATIONS

Ch, chain; dc, double crochet; st, stitch; tr, treble; dtr, double treble; ttr, triple treble; slst, slip st; chsp, chain space.

TO MAKE

With 3.50 hook and Darling Bud, make 7ch and slst into first ch to make a ring.

1st round: 3ch (counts as 1tr throughout), 19tr into ring, slst in top of 3ch – 20 sts.

2nd round: 1ch, 2dc in next st, [1tr in next st, 2tr in following st] 8 times, 1tr in next st, 2dc in last st, slst in 1ch.

3rd round: 1ch, 2dc in next st, 1tr in following st, 2tr in each of next 4 sts, 1tr in next st, 1dc in each of next 5 sts, 2tr in each of following 2 sts, then work 1tr, 1dtr and 1tr all in next st for base of heart, 2tr in each of next 2 sts, 1dc in each of following 5 sts, 1tr in next st, 2tr in each of following 4 sts, 1tr in next st, 2dc in last st, slst in 1ch. Fasten off.

4th round: Join Bluebird to top of dtr at base of heart, 1ch, 1dc in dtr, 1dc in each of next 22 sts, 1dc in 1ch at beginning of 2nd round (2 rounds below) for centre st, 1dc in each of next 22 sts, 1dc in same dtr at base of heart, slst in 1ch.

5th round: 1ch, 1dc in each of next 2 sts, 1tr in each of following 2 sts, 1dtr in next st, work 1ttr, 1ch and 1ttr all in following st, 1dtr in next st, 1tr in each of following 2 sts, 1dc in each of next 6 sts, 1tr in each of following 2 sts, work 1dtr, 1ch and 1dtr all in next st, 1tr in following st, 1dc in each of next 3 sts, 1tr in following st, 1tr in centre top st, 1tr in following st, 1dc in each of next 3 sts, 1tr in following st, work 1dtr, 1ch and 1dtr all in next st, 1tr in each of next 2 sts, 1dc in each of following 6 sts, 1tr in ech of next 2 sts, 1dtr in following st, work 1ttr, 1ch and 1ttr all in next st, 1dtr in following st, 1tr in each of next 2 sts, 1dc in following 2 sts, slst in 1ch.

6th round: Slst along and into first corner chsp, 2ch, 1dc in same chsp as slst, 1dc in each of next 13 sts, [work 1dc, 1ch and 1dc all in corner chsp, 1dc in each of next 13 sts] 3 times, slst in 1st of 2ch. Fasten off.

Make 4 more motifs in same way.

Make 5 more motif using Lotus instead of Darling Bud.

Make 5 more motif using Hot Pink instead of Darling Bud.

Make 5 more motif using Sapling instead of Darling Bud.

Make 5 more motif using Cool Aqua instead of Darling Bud.

TO MAKE UP

Arrange motifs in 5 rows of 5 motifs each and join as follows:

With base of one heart to top of second heart, place 2 motifs with backs together, having right sides facing. Join in Bluebird to right corner, and using 3.50 hook, insert hook through the top of matching stitches on both motifs at once, work a row of dc to join 2 straight edges. Join strip motifs in this way, then join the strips together, side by side to match.

Edging: With right sides facing and using 3.00 hook, rejoin Bluebird and work in crab stitch (dc worked from left to right) all round outer edge, working 2 sts into each corner.

Heart Cushion

This comfy, colourful cushion has a bright heart motif to cheer up any space

DIFFICULTY
✕ ✕ ✕ ✕

WHAT YOU NEED
• 4.00 crochet hook
• 40 x 40cm cushion pad
• 9 buttons in assorted contrasting shade
• DMC Woolly (100% wool)

Colour 1: 4 x 50g (125m) Dark Pink (055)
Colour 2: 1 x 50g (125m) Light Pink (042)
Colour 3: 1 x 50g (125m) Light Orange (012)
Colour 4: 1 x 50g (125m) Mid Pink (043)
Colour 5: 1 x 50g (125m) Light Blue (073)
Colour 6: 1 x 50g (125m) Mid Green (077)
Colour 7: 1 x 50g (125m) Royal Blue (075)
Colour 8: 1 x 50g (125m) Bright Orange (103)
Colour 9: 1 x 50g (125m) Lime Green (081)
Colour 10: 1 x 50g (125m) Mustard (091)

MEASUREMENTS
Approximately 40 x 40cm/16 x 16in.

TENSION
18 stitches and 8.5 rows to 10 x 10cm, over trebles, using 4.00 hook.

ABBREVIATIONS
Ch, chain; st, stitch; dc, double crochet; tr, treble; slst, slip st; chsp, chain space.

BACK AND FRONT (BOTH ALIKE)

With 4.00 hook and Dark Pink, make 68ch.

Foundation row: 1tr in 4th ch from hook (counts as 2tr), [1tr in next ch] to end, turn – 66tr.

Pattern row: 3ch (counts as 1tr), [1tr in next tr] to end, turn.

Pattern another 30 rows. Fasten off.

LARGE SQUARE MOTIFS (MAKE 1 IN EACH OF 9 SHADES)

1st round: With 4.00 hook and chosen shade, wind yarn round index finger of left hand to form a ring, insert hook into ring, yarn round hook and pull through, 3ch (counts as 1tr), work 11tr in ring, slst in top of 3ch, then pull end tightly to close ring – 12tr.

2nd round: 6ch (counts as 1tr and 3ch), 1tr in base of 6ch, 1tr in each of next 2tr, [work 1tr, 3ch and 1tr all in next tr, 1tr in each of next 2tr] to end, slst in 3rd of 6ch.

3rd round: Slst in next 3-chsp, 3ch (counts as 1tr), work 1tr, 3ch and 2tr all in same place as slst, 1tr in each of next 4tr, [work 2tr, 3ch and 2tr all in next 3-chsp, 1tr in each of next 4tr] to end, slst in top of 3ch.

4th round: 3ch (counts as 1tr), 1tr in next tr, [work 2tr, 3ch and 2tr all in next 3-chsp, 1tr in each of next 8tr] 3 times, work 2tr, 3ch and 2tr all in last 3-chsp, 1tr in last of last 6tr, slst into top of 3ch. Fasten off.

SMALL SQUARE MOTIFS (MAKE 1 IN EACH OF 9 SHADES)

Work 1st to 3rd rounds as given for large square motifs. Fasten off.

HEART MOTIFS (MAKE 1 IN EACH OF 9 SHADES)

1st round: With 4.00 hook and chosen shade, wind yarn round index finger of left hand to form a ring, insert hook into ring, yarn round hook and pull through, 3ch (counts as 1tr), work 11tr in ring, slst in top of 3ch, then pullend tightly to close ring – 12tr.

2nd round: 2ch, 2tr in each of next 5tr, 1tr in next tr, 2ch, slst in first of 2ch, 1tr in same place as last tr, 2tr in each of next 5tr, 2ch, slst in base of 2ch at beginning. Fasten off.

TO MAKE UP

Arrange large squares, evenly spaced on front of cushion and sew in place. Varying shades, sew small squares on top of large squares and heart motif on top of small squares. Sew a button in centre of each heart motif. With wrong sides together, using 4.00 hook and Dark Pink, crochet front and back pieces together, working a round of dc evenly around outer edges of back and front, leaving an opening. Insert cushion pad and close opening.

PATTERN NOTES

• Yarn amounts are based on average requirements and are therefore approximate. Instructions in square brackets are worked as stated after 2nd bracket.

Seat Cover

This lively seat cover will update dining chairs

TO MAKE

With 4.50 hook and Fuchsia, make 5ch and join with a slst to form a ring.

1st round: 5ch (counts as 1tr and 2ch throughout), [work 4tr in ring, 2ch] 3 times, 3tr in ring, slst in 3rd of 5ch – 4 groups of 4tr, with chsp at corners.
Fasten off.

2nd round: Join Aqua to first chsp, 5ch, 4tr in same chsp as join, [work 4tr, 2ch and 4tr in corner chsp] 3 times, 3tr in first chsp, slst in 3rd of 5ch – 8 groups.
Fasten off.

3rd round: Join Jade to first chsp, 5ch, 4tr in same chsp as join, [4tr in next space between 4tr groups, work 4tr, 2ch and 4tr in next corner chsp] 3 times, 4tr in next space between 4tr groups, 3tr in first chsp, slst in 3rd of 5ch – 12 groups. Fasten off.

4th round: Join Citrus to first chsp, 5ch, 4tr in same chsp as join, * [4tr in next space between 4tr groups] twice, work 4tr, 2ch and 4tr in next corner chsp, repeat from * twice more, [4tr in next space between 4tr groups] twice, 3tr in first chsp, slst in 3rd of 5ch – 16 groups.
Fasten off.

5th round: Join Fuchsia to first chsp, 5ch, 4tr in same chsp as join, * [4tr in next space between 4tr groups] 3 times, work 4tr, 2ch and 4tr all in next corner chsp, repeat from * twice more, [4tr in next space between 4tr groups] 3 times, 3tr in first chsp, slst in 3rd of 5ch – 20 groups.
Fasten off.

6th round: Join Aqua to first chsp, 5ch, 4tr in same chsp as join, * [4tr in next space between 4tr groups] 4 times, work 4tr, 2ch and 4tr all in next corner chsp, repeat from * twice more, [4tr in next space between 4tr groups] 4 times, 3tr in first chsp, slst in 3rd of 5ch – 24 groups.
Fasten off.

7th round: Join Jade to first chsp, 5ch, 4tr in same chsp as join, * [4tr in next space between 4tr groups] 5 times, work 4tr, 2ch and 4tr all in next corner chsp, repeat from * twice more, [4tr in next space between 4tr groups] 5 times, 3tr in first chsp, slst in 3rd of 5ch – 28 groups.
Fasten off.

DIFFICULTY	· Sharp scissors	MEASUREMENTS
✂ ✂ ✂ ✂	· Debbie Bliss Cotton DK (100% cotton)	Approximately 38 x 38cm/15 x 15in.
	Colour 1: 1 x 50g (84m) Fuchsia (58)	
WHAT YOU NEED	Colour 2: 1 x 50g (84m) Aqua (61)	ABBREVIATIONS
· 4.50 crochet hook	Colour 3: 1 x 50g (84m) Jade (78)	Ch, chain; st, stitch; dc, double crochet; tr, treble;
· Piece of stiff card 10 x 15cmk	Colour 4: 1 x 50g (84m) Citrus (79	chsp, chain space; slst, slip stitch.

8th round: Join Citrus to first chsp, 5ch, 4tr in same chsp as join, * [4tr in next space between 4tr groups] 6 times, work 4tr, 2ch and 4tr all in next corner chsp, repeat from * twice more, [4tr in next space between 4tr groups] 6 times, 3tr in first chsp, slst in 3rd of 5ch – 32 groups. Fasten off.

9th round: Join Fuchsia to first chsp, 5ch, 4tr in same chsp as join, * [4tr in next space between 4tr groups] 7 times, work 4tr, 2ch and 4tr all in next corner chsp, repeat from * twice more, [4tr in next space between 4tr groups] 7 times, 3tr in first chsp, slst in 3rd of 5ch – 36 groups. Fasten off.

10th round: Join Aqua to first chsp, 5ch, 4tr in same chsp as join, * [4tr in next space between 4tr groups] 8 times, work 4tr, 2ch and 4tr all in next corner chsp, repeat from * twice more, [4tr in next space between 4tr group] 8 times, 3tr in first chsp, slst in 3rd of 5ch – 40 groups. Fasten off.

11th round: Join Jade to first chsp, 5ch, 4tr in same chsp as join, * [4tr in next space between 4tr groups] 9 times, work 4tr, 2ch and 4tr all in next corner chsp, repeat from * twice more, [4tr in next space between 4tr groups] 9 times, 3tr in first chsp, slst in 3rd of 5ch – 44 groups. Fasten off.

12th round: Join Citrus to first chsp, 5ch, 4tr in same chsp as join, * [4tr in next space between 4tr groups] 10 times, work 4tr, 2ch and 4tr all in next corner chsp, repeat from * twice more, [4tr in next space between 4tr groups] 10 times, 3tr in first chsp, slst in 3rd of 5ch – 48 groups. Fasten off.

13th round: Join in Fuchsia to first chsp, 5ch, 4tr in same chsp as join, * [4tr in next space between 4tr groups] 11 times, work 4tr, 2ch and 4tr all in next corner chsp, repeat from * twice more, [4tr in next space between 4tr groups] 11 times, 3tr in first chsp, slst in 3rd of 5ch – 52 groups. Fasten off.

14th round: Join in Aqua to first chsp, 5ch, 4tr in same chsp as join, * [4tr in next space between 4tr groups] 12 times, work 4tr, 2ch and 4tr all in next corner chsp, repeat from * twice more, [4tr in next space between 4tr groups] 12 times, 3tr in first chsp, slst in 3rd of 5ch – 56 groups. Fasten off.

Edging round: Join in Jade to first chsp, 1ch, 1dc in same place as join, 1ch, * [4tr in next space between 4tr groups] 13 times, 1ch, 1dc in next chsp, 1ch, repeat from * twice more, [4tr in next space between 4tr groups] 13 times, 1ch, slst in first dc. Fasten off.

PLAITED TIES WITH TASSELS

Ties (make 8): For each tie, cut 3 x 60cm lengths from 3 different shades. Fold in half, pin centre to a cushion and plait firmly for 18cm. Fasten off securely with an overhand knot and trim loose ends to 2cm.

Tassels (make 8): First, divide remaining shades into 8 equal parts. Take one strand of each colour together and wind around centre of card about 35 times. With sharp scissors, cut yarn through all thicknesses on one side of card. Lay strands flat and use one strand of Fuchsia to tie them together securely around middle.

Fold strands in half. Take one plaited tie and tuck knot into middle of strands so that plait comes out at the top of folded edge. To secure tassel, wrap Fuchsia around strands, about 2.5cm down from fold and fasten off securely. Trim ends of tassel to desired length.

Sew 2 plaited ties to each corner to create the tassels.

PATTERN NOTES

· Yarn amounts are based on average requirements and are therefore approximate. Instructions in square brackets are worked as stated after 2nd bracket.

Entrelac Pet Bed

A snuggly pet bed for your furry friend
to snooze in style

DIFFICULTY

✕ ✕ ✕ ✕

WHAT YOU NEED

- 6.00 Tunisian crochet hook or 18cm/7in long straight hook and a bung or point protector for the end
- 45¾ x 45¾cm/18 x 18in cushion pad
- Approximately 250g of fibre filling
- Optional zip 30cm/12in long
- Hayfield Bonus DK (100% acrylic)

Colour: 2 x 100g (280m) Raspberry (689)

- Hayfield Bonus Glitter DK (95% acrylic, 5% polyester)

Colour: 2 x 100g (296m) Grey (226)

MEASUREMENTS

Approximately 40 x 40cm/16 x 16in.

TENSION

2 x 2 entrelac blocks, to 10 x 10cm, over pattern, using 6.00 hook.

ABBREVIATIONS

Ch, chain ; st(s), stitch(es); dc, double crochet; slst, slip stitch; yrh, yarn round hook; tss, Tunisian simple stitch; bind off, miss first vertical bar at base of loop on hook, [insert hook under next vertical bar, yrh, pull loop through vertical bar and through loop on hook] to end.

PATTERN NOTES

- This project uses entrelac crochet with Tunisian simple stitch (tss) in 2 colours. Double crochet is used to join pieces. Entrelac crochet is a form of crochet that uses Tunisian techniques to create small diamond blocks. A centre block is made first, then more blocks are joined around the centre in rounds. With Tunisian crochet you do not turn the work, you work with the right side facing you at all times. Each row consists of picking up loops on one row, followed by a return row which involves taking the loops off the hook. The pet bed is constructed as a base cushion and 4 side cushions which are filled with fibre filling and crocheted together. Cords are added to the side cushion corners and tied together to create the bed shape. Yarn amounts are based on average requirements and are therefore approx. Instructions in square brackets are worked as stated after 2nd bracket.

BASE (MAKE 2 ALIKE)

Centre diamond block: With Grey, make 7ch.

1st row: Insert hook in 2nd ch from hook, yrh and pull loop through, [insert hook in next ch, yrh and pull loop through] 5 times (7 loops on hook), yrh and pull through 1 loop, [yrh and pull through 2 loops] 6 times (1 loop remains on hook) – 6 tss.

2nd row: Miss first vertical bar at base of ch on hook, [insert hook under next vertical bar, yrh and pull loop through] 5 times, insert hook under last vertical bar and through side of st at end of row, yrh and pull loop through (7 loops on hook), yrh and pull through 1 loop, [yrh and pull through 2 loops] 6 times (1 loop remains on hook) – 6 tss.
Repeat 2nd row another 4 times.

Next row: Bind off (1 loop remains on hook). Fasten off.

2nd round: With Raspberry, make 4 corner diamonds around the centre block, thus:

Corner diamond block: Join Raspberry to a corner of centre block and make 6ch.

1st row: Insert hook in 2nd ch from hook, yrh and pull through, [insert hook in next ch, yrh and pull loop through] 4 times, insert hook through edge st of adjoining block, yrh and pull loop through (7 loops on hook),

[yrh and pull through 2 loops] 6 times (1 loop remains on hook) – 6 tss.

2nd row: Miss first vertical bar at base of ch on hook, [insert hook under next vertical bar, yrh and pull loop through] 5 times, insert hook through edge st of adjoining block, yrh and pull loop through (7 loops on hook), [yrh and pull through 2 loops] 6 times (1 loop remains on hook) – 6 tss.
Repeat 2nd row another 4 times.

Next row: Bind off (1 loop remains on hook), insert hook through edge st of adjoining block, yrh and pull loop through edge st and through loop on hook (1 loop remains on hook). Fasten off.

Work 3 more corner diamonds in Raspberry for each corner of centre block.

3rd round: With Grey, make 8 blocks around the 2nd round, consisting of 4 fill blocks and 4 corner blocks, thus:

** Fill diamond block: Join Grey to top right corner of a block from previous round (to the start of the bind off row).

1st row: Insert hook through each st along top of block, yrh and pull loop through (6 loops on hook), insert hook through edge st of adjoining block, yrh and pull loop through (7 loops on hook), [yrh and pull through 2 loops] 6 times (1 loop remains on hook) – 6 tss.

2nd row: Miss first vertical bar at base of ch on hook, [insert hook under next vertical bar, yrh and pull loop through] 5 times, insert hook through edge st of adjoining block, yrh and pull loop through (7 loops on hook), [yrh and pull through 2 loops] 6 times (1 loop remains on hook) – 6 tss.
Repeat 2nd row another 4 times.

Next row: Bind off (1 loop remains on hook), insert hook through edge st of adjoining block, yrh and pull loop through edge st and through loop on hook (1 loop remains on hook). Fasten off.

Next, work a corner block following 2nd round instructions. **
Repeat from ** to ** 3 times more.

4th round: With Raspberry, work 12 blocks around 3rd round as [corner diamond and 2 fill diamonds] 4 times.

5th to 7th rounds: Continuing to alternate colours, work as for 4th round, adding an extra fill block between each corner block for each successive round.

Final round: The final round consists of triangles to 'square off' the diamond pattern. With Raspberry, make 6 triangles along each side, thus:

Triangle: Rejoin Raspberry to top right of a corner block from previous round.

1st row: Insert hook through each st along top of block, yrh and pull loop through (6 loops on hook), insert hook through edge st of adjoining block, yrh and pull loop through (7 loops on hook), [yrh and pull through 2 loops] 6 times (1 loop remains on hook) – 6 tss.

2nd row: Miss first vertical bar, insert hook under next 2 vertical bars, yrh and pull loop through, [insert hook under next vertical bar, yrh and pull loop through] 3 times (5 loops on hook), insert hook through edge st of adjoining block, yrh and pull loop through (6 loops on hook), [yrh and pull through 2 loops] 5 times (1 loop remains on hook) – 5 tss.

3rd row: Miss first vertical bar, insert hook under next 2 vertical bars, yrh and pull loop through, [insert hook under next vertical bar, yrh and pull loop through] twice (4 loops on hook), insert hook though edge st of adjoining block, yrh and pull loop through (5 loops on hook), [yrh and pull through 2 loops] 4 times (1 loop remains on hook) – 4 tss.

4th row: Miss first vertical bar, insert hook under next 2 vertical bars, yrh and pull loop through, insert hook under next vertical bar, yrh and pull loop through (3 loops on hook), insert hook though edge st of adjoining block, yrh and pull loop through (4 loops on hook), [yrh and pull through 2 loops] 3 times (1 loop remains on hook) – 3 tss.

5th row: Miss first vertical bar, insert hook under next 2 vertical bars, yrh and pull loop through, insert hook though edge st of adjoining block, yrh and pull loop through (3 loops on hook), [yrh and pull through 2 loops] twice (1 loop remains on hook) – 2 tss.

6th row: Miss first vertical bar, insert hook through next vertical bar and edge st together (2 loops on hook), yrh and pull through 2 loops (1 loop remains on hook), slst to top of the next block.

Repeat triangle along the fill blocks and at corner block. Fasten off. Rejoin yarn on other side of corner block and repeat the triangles along the remaining 3 sides of the base.

SIDES (MAKE 6 ALIKE)

Worked in rows in Tunisian simple stitch with 2 colours.
With Grey, make 51ch.

1st row: Insert hook in 2nd ch from hook, yrh and pull loop through, [insert hook in next ch, yrh and pull loop through] to end, drop Grey, do

not fasten off, join Raspberry, yrh and pull through 1 loop, [yrh and pull through 2 loops] to end – 50 sts.

2nd row: Continue with Raspberry, miss first vertical bar, [insert hook under next vertical bar, yrh and pull loop through] to last vertical bar, insert hook under last vertical bar and through side of st at end of row, drop Raspberry, do not fasten off, pick up Grey, yrh and pull through 1 loop, [yrh and pull through 2 loops] to end.

Repeat 2nd row another 18 times, changing colours at left side after picking up loops.

Next row: Bind off (1 loop remains on hook). Fasten off.

FRONT (MAKE 2 ALIKE)

Work as for sides to end of 6th row, fasten off colour not in use on left-hand side.

Right-hand side of front: Next row: Miss first vertical bar, [insert hook under next vertical bar, yrh and pull loop through] 12 times (13 loops on hook), drop Grey and join Raspberry, yrh and pull through 1 loop, [yrh and pull through 2 loops] to end.

Repeat 2nd row as given for sides, working over only 12 sts for another 13 rows.

Left-hand side of front: Next row: Rejoin Grey to 13th st of 6th row 6, bind off next 26 sts, pick up loops from next 12 vertical bars (including last bar and side of st), drop Grey, do not fasten off, rejoin Raspberry, yrh and pull through 1 loop, [yrh and pull through 2 loops] to end.

Repeat 2nd row as given for sides, working over only 12 sts for another 13 rows.

TO MAKE UP

First, place the front and back base pieces together with right sides facing outwards. Join the pieces using dc, working through both thicknesses around all 4 sides to join and inserting the cushion pad before joining the final side. If using a zip, join 3 sides and on the 4th side, leave an opening long enough for the zip. Position and pin zip then hand sew in place using small stitches. Next, place the 2 front pieces together with right sides facing outwards and dc around to join, working through both thicknesses and stuff with fibre fill as you go.

Next, place 2 side pieces together with right sides facing outwards, and dc around to join, working through both thicknesses and stuff with fibre fill as you go. Join the remaining side pieces in the same way.

Join sides and front to base, thus: Join each side piece to the base using dc. Do not fasten off after joining each side; simply continue along the next side. Next make 8 cords, thus: 1st row: Join yarn to top corner of any side piece with a slst, pick up loops through each of next 4 dc (5 loops on hook), yrh and pull through 1 loop, [yrh and pull through 2 loops] to end – 4 tss.

2nd row: Miss first vertical bar, pick up loop through each of next 4 vertical bars, (5 loops on hook) yrh and pull through 1 loop, [yrh and pull through 2 loops] to end. Repeat 2nd row another 28 times.

Fasten off. Sew each cord to the corner of each side piece and tie adjacent cords in a bow.

Snug for them and stylish for your home

Flat Pet Bed

Keep Fido comfy in trendy retro style

DIFFICULTY

✕ ✕ ✕ ✕

WHAT YOU NEED

- 6.00 crochet hook
- 66 x 66cm cushion pad for firm fit
- 50cm zip fastener
- Wendy Supreme Luxury Cotton Chunky
  (100% cotton)
  Colour 1: 4 x 100g (83m) Turquoise (36)
  Colour 2: 3 x 100g (83m) Teal (35)
  Colour 3: 1 x 100g (83m) Pink (33)
  Colour 4: 1 x 100g (83m) Rust (37)

Colour 5: 1 x 50g (125m) Deep Pink (38)

MEASUREMENTS

Approximately 48 x 52 x 10cm/19 x 20½ x 4in.

TENSION

13 stitches and 12 rows, to 10 x 10cm, over pattern, using
6.00 hook.

ABBREVIATIONS

Ch, chain; st, stitch; dc, double crochet; tr, treble; slst, slip st;
chsp, chain space.

BACK AND FRONT (BOTH ALIKE)

With 6.00 hook and Turquoise, make 62ch.
Foundation row (wrong side): 1dc in 4th ch from hook
(counts as chsp and 1dc) [1ch, miss next ch, 1dc in
next ch] to end, turn – 30chsp.
Pattern row: With Pink, work 2ch (counts as chsp),
[1dc in next chsp, 1ch, miss next dc] to last chsp, 1dc
in last chsp, turn.
Pattern another 62 rows in stripes of 1 row Teal, 1 row
Turquoise, 1 row Rust, 1 row Teal, 1 row Turquoise, 1
row Deep Pink, 1 row Teal, 1 row Turquoise and 1 row
Pink. Fasten off.

SIDE STRIP

With 6.00 hook and Turquoise, make 250ch.
Foundation row (wrong side): 1dc in 4th ch from hook
(counts as chsp and 1dc), [1ch, miss next ch, 1dc in
next ch] to end, turn – 124chsp.
Pattern row: With Turquoise, work 2ch (counts as
chsp), [1dc in next chsp, 1ch, miss next dc] to last
chsp, 1dc in last chsp, turn.

Pattern another 8 rows in stripes of 2 rows Teal, 2
rows Turquoise, 2 rows Teal and 2 rows Turquoise.
Fasten off.

TO MAKE UP

Join ends of side strip. With wrong sides together,
place side strip behind front and with 6.00 hook, join
Teal to corner of one short side, then and working
through both layers join front to side strip as follows:
Joining round: [1ch, 1dc in next chsp] to end. Fasten
off.
Join back to side strip in the same way on three
sides, leaving one long edge open for zip.
Work [1ch, 1dc in next chsp] along last edge of back.
Sew zip fastener in centre of opening, then close
opening at each side of fastener. Insert cushion pad.

PATTERN NOTES

• Yarn amounts are based on average requirements and are therefore approximate. Instructions in square brackets are worked as stated after 2nd bracket.

Lampshade

Cast a cosy glow with this crocheted number

DIFFICULTY

✕ ✕ ✕ ✕

WHAT YOU NEED

- 3.50 crochet hook
- Wilko 10in EDV Coolie lampshade
- A few marbles to weight base
  of lampshade

· Wendy Supreme Luxury Cotton 4-ply
(100% cotton)

Colour 1: 1 x 100g (267m) Peach (30)

Colour 2: 1 x 100g (267m) Mirage (44)

Colour 3: 1 x 100g (267m) Dragonfly (36)

Colour 4: 1 x 100g (267m) Beaujolais (35)

MEASUREMENTS

39cm/15¼in drop.

ABBREVIATIONS

Ch, chain; st, stitch; dc, double crochet; dtr, double
treble; slst, slip st; yrh, yarn round hook; dc2tog,
work 2 sts together thus: [insert hook in next st, yrh
and pull through] twice, yrh and pull through all 3
loops on hook.

TO MAKE

1st round: With 3.50 hook and Peach, wind yarn round index finger of left
hand to form a ring, insert hook into ring, yarn round hook and pull through,
1ch (does not count as a st throughout), work 6dc into ring, slst in first dc,
pull end tightly to close ring – 6dc. Break off Peach. Join in Mirage.

2nd round: 1ch, [2dc in next dc] to end, slst in first dc – 12dc. Break off
Mirage. Join in Peach.

3rd round: 1ch, [2dc in next dc, 1dc in next dc] to end, slst in first dc –
18dc. Break off Peach. Join in Mirage.

4th round: 4ch (counts as 1dtr throughout), [1dtr in next dc] to end, slst
in top of 4ch.

5th round: 1ch, [2dc in next dtr, 1dc in each of next 2dtr] to end, slst in
first dc – 24dc. Break off Mirage.

Join in Peach.

6th round: 1ch, [1dc in next dc] to end, slst in first dc. Break off Peach.
Join in Mirage.

7th round: 1ch, [2dc in next dc, 1dc in each of next 3dc] to end, slst in
first dc – 30dc.

8th round: As 4th round.

9th round: 1ch, [2dc in next dtr, 1dc in each of next 4dtr] to end, slst in
first dc – 36dc. Break off Mirage.

Join in Peach.

10th round: 1ch, [1dc in next dc] to end, slst in first dc. Break off Peach.
Join in Mirage.

11th round: 1ch, [2dc in next dc, 1dc in each of next 5dc] to end, slst in
first dc – 42dc.

12th round: As 4th round.

13th round: 1ch, [2dc in next dtr, 1dc in each of next 6dtr] to end, slst in
first dc – 48dc. Break off Mirage.

Join in Peach.

14th round: 1ch, [1dc in next dc] to end, slst in first dc. Break off Peach.
Join in Mirage.

15th round: 1ch, [2dc in next dc, 1dc in each of next 7dc] to end, slst in
first dc – 54dc.

16th round: As 4th round.

Break off Mirage. Join in Peach.

17th round: 1ch, [2dc in next dtr, 1dc in each of next 8dtr] to end, slst in
first dc – 60dc. Break off Peach.

Join in Dragonfly.

18th round: 1ch, [1dc in next dc] to end, slst in first dc. Break off
Dragonfly. Join in Peach.

19th round: 1ch, [2dc in next dc, 1dc in each of next 9dc] to end, slst in
first dc – 66dc.

20th round: As 4th round.

21st round: 1ch, [2dc in next dtr, 1dc in each of next 10dtr] to end, slst
in first dc – 72dc.

Break off Peach.

Join in Dragonfly.

22nd round: 1ch, [1dc in next dc] to end, slst in first dc. Break off
Dragonfly. Join in Peach.

23rd round: 1ch, [2dc in next dc, 1dc in each of next 11dc] to end, slst
in first dc – 78dc.

24th round: As 4th round.

25th round: 1ch, [2dc in next dtr, 1dc in each of next 12dtr] to end, slst in
first dc – 84dc. Break off Peach.

Join in Dragonfly.

26th round: 1ch, [1dc in next dc] to end, slst in first dc. Break off Dragonfly.
Join in Peach.

27th round: 1ch, [2dc in next dc, 1dc in each of next 13dc] to end, slst in first dc – 90dc.

28th round: As 4th round.

29th round: 1ch, [2dc in next dtr, 1dc in each of next 14dtr] to end, slst in first dc – 96dc. Break off Peach.

Join in Dragonfly.

30th round: 1ch, [1dc in next dc] to end, slst in first dc. Break off Dragonfly. Join in Peach.

31st round: 1ch, [2dc in next dc, 1dc in each of next 15dc] to end, slst in first dc – 102dc.

32nd round: As 4th round.

Break off Peach. Join in Dragonfly.

33rd round: 1ch, [2dc in next dtr, 1dc in each of next 16dtr] to end, slst in first dc – 108dc. Break off Dragonfly.

Join in Mirage.

34th round: 1ch, [1dc in next dc] to end, slst in first dc. Break off Mirage. Join in Dragonfly.

35th round: 1ch, [2dc in next dc, 1dc in each of next 17dc] to end, slst in first dc – 114dc.

36th round: As 4th round.

37th joining round: Remove shade from wire lamp shade frame. Work dc around outer edge of larger wire ring of lampshade frame thus: 1ch, [insert hook in next dtr, yrh and pull loop through, taking loop to top of wire, yrh and pull through 2 loops on hook] to end, slst in first dc. Break off Dragonfly. Join in Mirage.

38th round: 1ch, [1dc in next dc] to end, slst in first dc. Break off Mirage. Join in Dragonfly.

39th round: 1ch, [dc2tog, 1dc in each of next 17dc] to end, slst in first dc – 108dc.

40th round: As 4th round.

41st round: 1ch, [dc2tog, 1dc in each of next 16dtr] to end, slst in first dc – 102dc.

Break off Dragonfly. Join in Mirage.

42nd round: 1ch, [1dc in next dc] to end, slst in first dc. Break off Mirage. Join in Dragonfly.

43rd round: 1ch, [dc2tog, 1dc in each of next 15dc] to end, slst first dc – 96dc.

Break off Dragonfly. Join in Mirage.

44th round: As 4th round.

45th round: 1ch, [dc2tog, 1dc in each of next 14dtr] to end, slst in first dc – 90dc. Break off Mirage. Join in Beaujolais.

46th round: 1ch, [1dc in next dc] to end, slst in first dc. Break off Beaujolais. Join in Mirage.

47th round: 1ch, [dc2tog, 1dc in each of next 13dc] to end, slst in first cdc – 84dc.

48th round: As 4th round.

49th round: 1ch, [dc2tog, 1dc in each of next 12dtr] to end, slst in first dc – 78dc.

Break off Mirage. Join in Beaujolais.

50th round: 1ch, [1dc in next dc] to end, slst in first dc. Break off Beaujolais.

Join in Mirage.

51st round: 1ch, [dc2tog, 1dc in each of next 11dc] to end, slst in first dc – 72dc.

52nd round: As 4th round.

53rd round: 1ch, [dc2tog, 1dc in each of next 10dtr] to end, slst in first dc – 66dc.

Break off Mirage. Join in Beaujolais.

54th round: 1ch, [1dc in next dc] to end, slst in first dc. Break off Beaujolais.

Join in Mirage.

55th round: 1ch, [dc2tog, 1dc in each of next 9dc] to end, slst in first dc – 60dc.

56th round: As 4th round.

57th round: 1ch, [dc2tog, 1dc in each of next 8dtr] to end, slst in first dc – 54dc.

58th joining round: Working dc around smaller wire ring of lampshade frame, work as given for 37th joining round. Fasten off.

To keep shade taut, place a few marbles in base of lampshade.

PATTERN NOTES

• Yarn amounts are based on average requirements and are therefore approximate. Instructions in square brackets are worked as stated after 2nd bracket.

Trio of Baskets

Little baskets for odds and ends

DIFFICULTY

✕ ✕ ✕ ✕

WHAT YOU NEED

• 3.50 crochet hook
• Wendy Supreme Luxury Cotton 4-ply (100% cotton)

Colour 1: 2 x 100g (267m) Mirage (44)
Colour 2: 1 x 100g (267m) Orchid (37)
Colour 3: 1 x 100g (267m) Dragonfly (36)
Colour 4: 1 x 100g (267m) Beaujolais (35)
Colour 5: 1 x 100g (267m) Peach (30)

MEASUREMENTS

Approximately 15cm/6in diameter x 8.5cm/3¼in tall.

ABBREVIATIONS

Ch, chain; st, stitch; dc, double crochet; chsp, chain space; slst, slip st.

BASKET ONE

1st round: With 3.50 hook and Mirage, wind yarn round index finger of left hand to form a ring, insert hook into ring, yarn round hook and pull through, 1ch (does not count as a st throughout), work 6dc into ring, slst in first dc – 6dc. Mark end of last round and move marker up at end of every round.

2nd round: [2dc in next st] 6 times – 12dc.

3rd round: [2dc in next dc, 1dc in next dc] 6 times – 18dc.

4th round: [2dc in next dc, 1dc in each of next 2dc] 6 times – 24dc.

5th round: [2dc in next dc, 1dc in each of next 3dc] 6 times – 30dc.

6th round: [2dc in next dc, 1dc in each of next 4dc] 6 times – 36dc.

7th round: [2dc in next dc, 1dc in each of next 5dc] 6 times – 42dc.

8th round: [2dc in next dc, 1dc in each of next 6dc] 6 times – 48dc.

9th round: [2dc in next dc, 1dc in each of next 7dc] 6 times – 54dc.

10th round: [2dc in next dc, 1dc in each of next 8dc] 6 times – 60dc.

11th round: [2dc in next dc, 1dc in each of next 9dc] 6 times – 66dc.

12th round: [2dc in next dc, 1dc in each of next 10dc] 6 times – 72dc.

13th round: [2dc in next dc, 1dc in each of next 11dc] 6 times – 78dc.

14th round: [2dc in next dc, 1dc in each of next 12dc] 6 times – 84dc.

15th round: [2dc in next dc, 1dc in each of next 13dc] 6 times – 90dc.

16th round: [2dc in next dc, 1dc in each of next 14dc] 6 times – 96dc.

17th round: [2dc in next dc, 1dc in each of next 15dc] 6 times – 102dc.

18th round: [2dc in next dc, 1dc in each of next 16dc] 6 times – 108dc.

19th round: [2dc in next dc, 1dc in each of next 17dc] 6 times – 114dc.

20th round: [2dc in next dc, 1dc each of next 18dc] 6 times, slst in first dc – 120dc.

21st round: Working in back loop only, work 1ch, [dc2tog, 1dc in each of next 18dc] 6 times, slst in first st – 114dc.

22nd round: 1ch, 1dc in base of ch, [1ch, miss next dc, 1dc in next dc] to last dc, 1ch, miss last dc, slst in first dc – 57dc. Break off Mirage. Join Peach in first chsp.

* 23rd round: 1ch, 1dc in base of 1ch, [1ch, miss next dc, 1dc in next chsp] to end, 1ch, slst in first dc.
Break off Peach.
Join Mirage in first chsp.

24th round: As 23rd round.
Break off Mirage.
Join Dragonfly in first chsp.

25th round: As 23rd round.
Break off Dragonfly.
Join Mirage in first chsp.

26th round: As 23rd round.
Break off Mirage.
Join Peach in first chsp. *

Work from * to *, 4 times more, then work 23rd row again.
Continue in Peach.

Next 5 rounds: 1ch, 1dc in first chsp, [1ch, miss next dc, 1dc in next chsp] to end, 1ch, slst in first dc. Fasten off.
Allow top rounds to roll on to right side.

BASKET TWO

Work as basket one, using Beaujolais instead of Peach and Peach instead of Dragonfly.

BASKET THREE

Work as basket one, using Orchid instead of Peach and Beaujolais instead of Dragonfly.

PATTERN NOTES

• Yarn amounts are based on average
  requirements and are therefore
  approximate. Instructions in square
  brackets are worked as stated after
  2nd bracket.

Clothes Care

Gentle hangers for delicate outfits

DIFFICULTY

✕ ✕ ✕ ✕

WHAT YOU NEED

• 4.00 crochet hook
• 2 x 30cm-wide wooden coat hangers
• Erika Knight Gossypium Cotton (100% cotton)

Colour 1: 1 x 50g (100m) Blue (504)
Colour 2: 1 x 50g (100m) Yellow (503)
Colour 3: 1 x 50g (100m) Cream (500)

ABBREVIATIONS

Ch, chain; dc, double crochet; st, stitch; chsp, chain space; slst, slip stitch; yrh, yarn round hook.

FRONT

With 4.00 hook and Blue, make 68ch.

Foundation row: 1dc in 2nd ch from hook, [1ch, miss 1ch, 1dc in next ch] 32 times, 1ch, miss 1ch, insert hook in last ch, yrh and pull through, change to Yellow, yrh and pull through 2 loops on hook, turn.

1st row: With Yellow, 1ch (does not count as a st), 1dc in first dc, [1dc in next chsp, 1ch, miss next dc] to last chsp, 1dc in last chsp, insert hook in last dc, yrh and pull through, change to Cream, yrh and pull through 2 loops on hook, turn.

2nd row: With Cream, 1ch (does not count as a st), 1dc in first dc, [1ch, miss next dc, 1dc in next chsp] to last 2dc, 1ch, miss next dc, insert hook in last dc, yrh and pull through, change to Blue, yrh and pull through 2 loops on hook, turn.

3rd row: Using Blue instead of Yellow and Yellow instead of Cream, work as 1st row.

4th row: Using Yellow instead of Cream and Cream instead of Blue, work as 2nd row.

5th row: Using Cream instead of Yellow, and Blue instead of Cream, work as 1st rows.

6th row: With Blue only, work as 2nd row, but do not turn.

Edging round: Work another 2dc in same place as last dc of 6th row, 3dc evenly spaced along row-ends to corner, 3dc in corner, 51dc along chain edge, 3dc in corner, 3dc along other row-ends, 3dc in corner, then

51dc along top edge, slst in first dc. Fasten off.

BACK

Using Blue only, work as given for front.

TO MAKE UP

Place front and back with wrong sides together and right side of front facing, join Blue to centre of 3dc at bottom right corner and working through both layers slst in each st to centre of top edge, place cover over hanger and continue to work slst through both layers along top edge, then short side edge, slst in corner dc, [3ch, miss 1 st, slst in next st on both layers] along bottom edge to last st, 3ch, miss last st, slst in same place as first slst. Fasten off.

Make another cover for hanger, using Cream instead of Blue and Blue instead of Cream.

PATTERN NOTES

• Yarn amounts are based on average requirements and are therefore approximate. Instructions in square brackets are worked as stated after 2nd bracket.

Tartan Touch

Our graphic plaid cushion looks great teamed with florals

DIFFICULTY

✕ ✕ ✕ ✕

WHAT YOU NEED

• 4.00 crochet hook
• Epsom salts for stiffening
• Erika Knight Gossypium Cotton (100% cotton)

Colour 1: 5 x 50g (100m) Milk (500)
Colour 2: 5 x 50g (100m) Sea Fret (501)

MEASUREMENTS

Approximately 26cm/10¼in wide and 16cm/6½in deep at base and 12.5cm/5in high.

ABBREVIATIONS

Ch, chain; st, stitch; dc, double crochet; spike st, insert hook into top of next st two rows below, yarn over hook and pull through, yarn over hook and pull through all 2 loops on hook.

BACK

Square (make 4): With 5.50 hook and using two strands of Glacier together, make 13ch.

1st row: 1dc in 2nd ch from hook, [1dc in next ch] 11 times, turn – 12dc.

2nd to 13th rows: 1ch (does not count as a st throughout instructions), [1dc in next dc] 12 times, turn. Fasten off.

Top edge border: With right side facing and using 5.50 hook, join one strand of Glacier and one strand of Kingfisher to top right corner of square.

1st row: 1ch, 1dc in same place as join, [1dc in next dc] 11 times, turn – 12dc.

2nd to 4th rows: 1ch, [1dc in next dc] 12 times, turn. Fasten off.

Left side border: With right side facing and using 5.50 hook, join one strand of Glacier and one strand of Kingfisher to corner at beginning of last row worked.

1st row: 1ch, 1dc in same place as join, work 15dc evenly along edge, turn – 16dc.

2nd to 4th rows: 1ch, [1dc in next dc] 16 times, turn. Fasten off.

Bottom edge border: With right side facing and using 5.50 hook, join one strand of Glacier and one strand of Kingfisher to corner at beginning of last row worked.

1st row: 1ch, 1dc in same place as join, 1dc in each of next 3 row-ends, [1dc in next base ch] 12 times, turn – 16 sts.

2nd to 4th rows: 1ch, [1dc in next dc] 16 times, turn. Fasten off.

Right side border: With right side facing and using 5.50 hook, join one strand of Glacier and one strand of Kingfisher to corner at beginning of last row worked.

1st row: 1ch, 1dc in same place as join, work 19dc evenly along edge, turn – 20dc.

2nd to 4th rows: 1ch, [1dc in next dc] 20 times, turn. Fasten off.

Edging: With right side facing and using 5.50 hook, join two strands of Kingfisher to any corner of square.

1st round: 1ch, 3dc in same place as join, [work 18dc along one edge, 3dc in next corner] 3 times, work 18dc along last edge, slst in first dc – 84dc.

2nd round: 1ch, 1dc in same place as slst, [3dc in next dc, 1dc in each of next 20dc] 4 times, ending last repeat with 19dc instead of 20, slst in first dc. Fasten off.

Join squares: Lay squares flat in 2 rows of 2 square each, with top edge borders all facing in same direction. Using one strand of Kingfisher and tapestry needle, work whip stitches along back loops only to join the 4 squares together.

Final round: With right side facing, using 5.50 hook and two strands of Kingfisher together, work a round of dc evenly around outer edges, working 3dc in centre dc at each corner and 1htr at each join, slst in first dc. Fasten off and neaten all ends.

Using photo as guide, with one strand of Dusky Pink and tapestry needle, work 3 horizontal lines of chain stitches at top and bottom, plus 2 vertical lines at each side.

FRONT

Work as back, using Dusky Pink instead of Kingfisher and Kingfisher instead of Dusky Pink, except on final round, use one strand of Glacier and one strand of Kingfisher together.

TO MAKE UP

With wrong sides together, using 5.50 hook and one strand of Kingfisher, join outer edges, working slst in back loops only, leaving an opening. Insert cushion pad and close opening.

PATTERN NOTES

• Yarn amounts are based on average requirements and are therefore approximate. Instructions in square brackets are worked as stated after 2nd bracket.

PATTERN NOTES

- Yarn amounts are based on average requirements and are therefore approximate. Instructions in square brackets are worked as stated after 2nd bracket.

Crochet Baskets

Stylish storage in cool colours that are versatile all around the house

---

DIFFICULTY

✕ ✕ ✕ ✕

WHAT YOU NEED

- 4.00 crochet hook
- Epsom salts for stiffening
- Erika Knight Gossypium (100% cotton)

Colour 1: 5 x 50g (100m) Milk (500)
Colour 2: 5 x 50g (100m) Sea Fret (501)

MEASUREMENTS

Approx. 26cm/10¼in wide and 16cm/6½in deep at base and 12.5cm/5in high.

ABBREVIATIONS

Ch, chain; st, stitch; dc, double crochet; chsp, chain space; slst, slip st.

BASE

With 4.00 hook and Sea Fret, make 46ch.

Foundation row: 1dc in 2nd ch from hook (counts as 1 st), [1dc in next ch] to end, turn – 45 sts.

1st to 30th rows: 1ch (does not count as a st throughout), [1dc in next st] to end, turn. Fasten off.

BACK AND FRONT (BOTH ALIKE)

With 4.00 hook and Milk, make 46ch.

Foundation row: 1dc in 2nd ch from hook, [1dc in next ch] to end, turn – 45 sts.

1st to 5th rows: 1ch, [1dc in next st] to end, turn. Break off Milk. Join in Sea Fret.

6th row: 1ch, 2dc in first st, [spike st in next st, 1dc in next st] to last 2 sts, spike st in next st, 2dc into last st, turn – 47 sts.

7th to 12th rows: 1ch, [1dc in next st] to end, turn. Break off Sea Fret. Join in Milk.

13th row: As 6th row – 49 sts.

14th to 19th rows: As 7th to 12th rows. Break off Milk. Join in Sea Fret.

20th row: As 6th row – 51 sts.

21st to 26th rows: As 7th to 12th rows. Break off Sea Fret. Join in Milk.

27th row: 1ch, [1dc in next st, spike st in next st] to last st, 1dc in last st. Fasten off.

SIDES (MAKE 2)

With 4.00 hook and Milk, make 32ch.

Foundation row: 1dc in 2nd ch from hook, [1dc in next ch] to end, turn – 31dc.

1st to 5th rows: 1ch, [1dc in next st] to end, turn. Break off Milk. Join in Sea Fret.

6th row: 1ch, 2dc in first dc, [spike st in next st, 1dc in next st] to last 2 sts, spike st in next st, 2dc in last st, turn – 33 sts.

7th to 12th rows: 1ch, [1dc in next st] to end, turn. Break off Sea Fret. Join in Milk.

13th row: As 6th row – 35 sts.

14th to 19th rows: As 7th to 12th rows. Break off Milk. Join in Sea Fret.

20th row: As 6th row, turn – 37 sts.

21st to 26th rows: As 7th to 12th rows. Break off Sea Fret. Join in Milk.

27th row: 1ch, [1dc in next st, spike st in next st] to last st, 1dc in last st. Fasten off.

TO MAKE UP

Using 4.00 hook and Sea Fret, with wrong sides together and base at back, join chain edges of back, front and sides to base by working a round of dc evenly along each piece and base edges.

Join side seams. To stiffen, mix equal parts of Epsom salts and boiling water in a large bowl and stir.

When water has cooled, immerse basket in mixture, remove and pull into shape, then leave to dry and stiffen.

Make another two baskets as given for striped basket, but working one in Milk and the other in Sea Fret.

Jewellery Box

A pretty place to keep your favourite jewellery

DIFFICULTY

✕ ✕ ✕ ✕

WHAT YOU NEED

• 2.50 crochet hook
• 108 gold metal round beads
• 108 gold glass bugle beads
• Sewing needle and matching sewing thread
• Stout card

• Pair of compasses and pencil
• Ruler and glue
• DMC Petra 3 (100% cotton)
  Colour: 1 x 100g (280m) Camel (53045)
• DMC Mouline embroidery thread
  Colour: 1 (8m) skein Camel (E436)

MEASUREMENTS

Approximately 11.5cm/4½in in diameter and

6.5cm/2½in high.

ABBREVIATIONS

Ch, chain; st, stitch; dc, double crochet; tr, treble; slst, slip stitch; fpdtr, yarn round hook twice, take hook from front to back, around post of next st then to front again, yarn round hook and pull through, [yarn round hook and pull through first 2 loops on hook] 3 times.

BASE

Inner bottom: 1st round: With 2.50 hook, wind yarn around index finger of left hand to form a slip ring, insert hook in ring, yarn round hook and pull through, 1ch (counts as 1 st), work 11dc in ring, slst in 1ch then pull end up tightly to close ring – 12 sts.

2nd round: 3ch (counts as 1tr), [3tr in next st, 1tr in next st] 5 times, 3tr in last st, slst in 3rd of 3ch – 24 sts.

3rd round: 3ch (counts as 1tr), 1tr in next st, [3tr in next st, 1tr in each of next 3 sts] 5 times, 3tr in next st, 1tr in last st, slst in 3rd of 3ch – 36 sts.

4th round: 3ch (counts as 1tr), 1tr in each of next 2 sts, [3tr in next st, 1tr in each of next 5 sts] 5 times, 3tr in next st, 1tr each of last 2 sts, slst in 3rd of 3ch – 48 sts.

5th round: 3ch (counts as 1tr), 1tr in each of next 3 sts, [3tr in next st, 1tr in each of next 7 sts] 5 times, 3tr in next st, 1tr each of last 3 sts, slst in 3rd of 3ch – 60 sts.

6th round: 3ch (counts as 1tr), 2tr in base of 3ch, [1tr in each of next 9 sts, 3tr in next st] 5 times, 1tr each of last 9 sts, slst in 3rd of 3ch – 72 sts. ** Fasten off.

Outer bottom: Work as inner bottom to **.

Place outer and inner bottom pieces with wrong sides together and insert smaller disc between them. With outer bottom facing, join bottom pieces together by working 1ch, 1dc in each pair of corresponding sts from both layers to end, slst in 1ch.

Inner sides: 1st round: With outer bottom facing, 3ch (counts as 1tr), working in back loop of every st, [1tr in next st] to end, slst in 3rd of 3ch – 72 sts. Mark this round.

2nd to 7th rounds: 3ch (counts as 1tr), [1tr in next st] to end, slst in 3rd of 3ch. Fasten off.

Outer sides: With outer bottom facing, join yarn to base of 3ch on marked round.

1st round: 3ch (counts as 1tr), working in front loop of every st, [1tr in next st] to end, slst in 3rd of 3ch – 72 sts.

2nd to 5th rounds: 3ch (counts as 1tr), [1fpdtr in next st, 1tr in each of next 5tr] 11 times, 1fpdtr in next st, 1tr in each of last 4tr, slst in 3rd of 3ch.

6th and 7th rounds: 3ch (counts as 1tr), [1tr in next st] to end, slst in 3rd of 3ch – 72 sts.

Insert larger ring between outer and inner sides and join side together by working 1ch, 1dc in each pair of corresponding sts from both layers to end, slst in 1ch. Fasten off.

LID

Inner top: 1st round: With 2.50 hook, make slip ring as on inner bottom of base, 1ch (counts as 1 st), work 11dc in ring, slst in 1ch then pull end up tightly to close ring – 12 sts.

2nd round: 3ch (counts as 1tr), [3tr in next st, 1tr in next st] 5 times, 3tr in last st, slst in 3rd of 3ch – 24 sts.

3rd round: 3ch (counts as 1tr), 1tr in next st, [3tr in next st, 1tr in each of next 3 sts] 5 times, 3tr in next st, 1tr in last st, slst in 3rd of 3ch – 35 sts.

4th round: 3ch (counts as 1tr), 1tr in each of next 2 sts, [3tr in next st, 1tr in each of next 5 sts] 5 times, 3tr in next st, 1tr each of last 2 sts, slst in 3rd of 3ch – 48 sts.

5th round: 3ch (counts as 1tr), 1tr in each of next 3 sts, [3tr in next st, 1tr in each of next 7 sts] 5 times, 3tr in next st, 1tr each of last 3 sts, slst in 3rd of 3ch – 60 sts.

6th round: 3ch (counts as 1tr), 2tr in base of 3ch, [1tr in each of next 9 sts, 3tr in next st] 5 times, 1tr in each of last 9 sts, slst in 3rd of 3ch – 72 sts.

7th round: 1ch (counts as 1 st), 3dc in next st, [1dc in each of next 11 sts, 3dc in next st] 5 times, 1dc in each of last 10 sts, slst in 1ch – 84 sts. Fasten off.

Outer top: 1st round: With 2.50 hook, make slip ring as on inner bottom of base, 3ch (counts as 1 st), work 23tr in ring, slst in 3rd of 3ch then pull end up tightly to close ring – 24 sts.

2nd round: 3ch (counts as 1tr), 1tr in base of 3ch, [1tr in next st, 2tr in next st, 1fpdtr, 2tr in next st] 5 times, 1tr in next st, 2tr in next st, 1fpdtr, slst in 3rd of 3ch – 36 sts.

3rd round: 3ch (counts as 1tr), 1tr in base of 3ch, [1tr in each of next 3 sts, 2tr in next st, 1fpdtr, 2tr in next st] 5 times, 1tr in each of next 3 sts, 2tr in next st, 1fpdtr, slst in 3rd of 3ch – 48 sts.

4th round: 3ch (counts as 1tr), 1tr in base of 3ch, [1tr in each of next 2 sts, 1fpdtr, 1tr in each of next 2 sts, 2tr in next st, 1fpdtr, 2tr in next st] 5 times, 1tr in each of next 2 sts, 1fpdtr, 1tr in each of next 2 sts, 2tr in next st, 1fpdtr, slst in 3rd of 3ch – 60 sts.

5th round: 3ch (counts as 1tr), 1tr in base of 3ch, [1tr in each of next 3 sts, 1fpdtr, 1tr in each of next 3 sts, 2tr in next st, 1fpdtr, 2tr in next st] 5 times, 1tr in each of next 3 sts, 1fpdtr, 1tr in each of next 3 sts, 2tr in next st, 1fpdtr, slst in 3rd of 3ch – 72 sts.

6th round: 3ch (counts as 1tr), 1tr in each of next 3 sts, [2tr in next st, 1fpdtr, 2tr in next st, 1tr in each of next 4 sts, 1fpdtr, 1tr in each next 4 sts] 5 times, 2tr in next st, 1fpdtr, 2tr in next st, 1tr in each of next 4 sts, 1fpdtr, slst in 3rd of 3ch – 84 sts.

Place outer and inner top pieces with wrong sides together and insert remaining disc between them. With outer top facing, join top pieces together by working 1ch, 1dc in each pair of corresponding sts from both layers to end, slst in 1ch.

Inner sides: 1st round: With outer top facing, 3ch (counts as 1tr), working in back loop of every st, [1tr in next st] to end, slst in 3rd of 3ch – 84 sts. Mark this round.

2nd round: 1ch, [1dc in next st] to end, slst in 1ch. Fasten off.

Outer side: With outer top facing, join yarn to base of 3ch on marked round.

1st round: 3ch (counts as 1tr), working in front loop of every st, [1tr in next st] to end, slst in 3rd of 3ch – 84 sts.

2nd round: 1ch, [1dc in next st] to end, slst in 1ch.

Insert remaining ring between outer and inner sides and join sides together by working 1ch, 1dc in each pair of corresponding sts from both layers to end, slst in 1ch. Fasten off.

TO COMPLETE

Sew 1 round bead at centre of each panel between fpdtr on sides of base, then sew 6 bugle beads around each round bead. Sew round beads to alternate stitches of joining round on lid sides and to top of alternate stitches of 6th round of lid top. Sew a round bead to start of each fpdtr ridge and a row of 3 bugle beads between each fpdtr ridge on lid top.

Using embroidery thread, make a tassel about 5cm long and attach to centre of lid top.

PATTERN NOTES

• Yarn amounts are based on average requirements and are therefore approximate. Instructions in square brackets are worked as stated after 2nd bracket.

Cushion Cover

A chic and colourful bolster-shaped cover to add interest to soft furnishings

DIFFICULTY

✕ ✕ ✕ ✕

WHAT YOU NEED

- 4mm crochet hook
- 50 x 100cm of lining fabric
- Sewing needle and matching thread
- 45cm fuchsia zip
- 45 x 17cm bolster cushion
- 2 matching tassels
- Sublime Extra Fine Merino Wool DK (100% wool)
  Colour 1: 4 x 50g (116m) Pink (485)
  Colour 2: 4 x 50g (116m) Green (487)

MEASUREMENTS

18 stitches and 8 rows, to 10 x 10cm, in body pattern, using 4mm hook.

TENSION

To fit a 45 x 17cm/17¾ x 6¾in bolster cushion.

ABBREVIATIONS

Ch, chain; st(s), stitch(es); tr, treble crochet; slst, slip stitch; chsp, chain space; ttr, triple treble crochet; dtr, double treble crochet.

CUSHION BODY

With 4mm hook and Pink, make 81ch.

1st row (right side): 2tr in 3rd ch from hook (the missed 2ch counts as 1tr), [4ch, miss 5 ch, 5tr in next ch] to end and working only 3tr at end of last repeat, turn.

2nd row: 2ch (counts as 1tr), miss first 3 sts, *(3tr, 3ch, 3tr) in next 4chsp**, miss next 5 tr, repeat from * ending last repeat at **, miss 2 tr, 1tr in top of turning ch, turn.

3rd row: 6ch (counts as 1ttr and 1ch), *5tr in next 3chsp**, 4ch, repeat from * ending last repeat at **, 1ch, 1ttr in top of turning ch, turn.

4th row: 5ch (counts as 1dtr and 1ch), 3tr in next 1chsp, *miss 5 tr, (3tr, 3ch, 3tr) in next 4chsp, repeat from * ending last repeat thus; miss 5 tr, (3tr, 1ch, 1dtr) in turning ch, turn.

5th row: 3ch (counts as 1tr), 2tr in next 1chsp, *4ch, 5tr in next 3chsp, repeat from * working last repeat thus; 4ch, 3tr in turning ch, turn.

Continue in pattern, repeating 2nd to 5th rows until body measures 55cm, finishing with either a 3rd or 5th row.

Fasten off.

CUSHION ENDS (MAKE 2 ALIKE)

With 4mm hook and Green, make 4ch, slst in first ch to make a ring.

Continue working in rounds with right side always facing.

1st round: 3ch (counts as first tr here and throughout instructions), 11tr into ring, slst in top of 3ch – 12 sts.

2nd round: 3ch, 1tr in st at base of 3ch, [2tr in next st] to end, slst in top of 3ch – 24 sts.

3rd round: 3ch, 2tr in next st, [1tr in next st, 2tr in next st] to end, slst in top of 3ch – 36 sts.

4th round: 3ch, 1tr in next st, 2tr in next st, [1tr in each of next 2 sts, 2tr in next st] to end, slst in top of 3ch – 48 sts.

5th round: 3ch, 1tr in each of next 2 sts, 2tr in next st, [1tr in each of next 3 sts, 2tr in next st] to end, slst in top of 3ch – 60 sts.

6th to 9th rounds: Continue in pattern as set, increasing the number of single tr sts between each increase by 1 tr on each round – 108 sts.

Fasten off.

TO MAKE UP

Cut lining fabric to 57 x 47cm and two circles of 19cm diameter (each piece includes 1cm for seam allowance). Stitch the zip to the rectangular piece along 47cm-edges to form a tube. Sew circular pieces to each tube end. Stitch top and bottom edges of crocheted body along edges of the zip. Sew circular crocheted ends around body edges. Add tassels.

PATTERN NOTES

• Yarn amounts are based on average requirements and are therefore approximate. Instructions in square brackets are worked as stated after 2nd bracket. Instructions in round brackets are all worked into the same st or space.

The lace pattern is placed over a lining fabric for a bold contrast

PATTERN NOTES

- Yarn amounts are based on average
  requirements and are therefore
  approximate. Instructions in square
  brackets are worked as stated after
  2nd bracket.

Cot Blanket & Bumper

Sweet dreams (almost) guaranteed

DIFFICULTY

✂ ✂ ✂ ✂

WHAT YOU NEED

Blanket
- Debbie Bliss Eco Baby (100% cotton)
  Colour: 5 x 50g (125m) Primrose (37)

Bumper
- Debbie Bliss Eco Baby (100% cotton)
  Colour: 5 x 50g (125m) Primrose (37)

Both items

- 3.50 and 4.00 crochet hooks

MEASUREMENTS

Blanket: 44 x 52.5cm/17¼ x 20½in.

Bumper: 100 x 22.5cm/39¼ x 8¾in.

TENSION

16 stitches and 10 rows, to 8 x 7.5cm, over pattern, using 4.00 hook.

ABBREVIATIONS

Ch, chain; dc, double crochet; st, stitch; htr, half treble; tr, treble; fptr, front post treble (yarn round hook, take hook from front to back, around post of next st then to front again, yarn round hook and pull through, [yarn round hook and pull through first 2 loops on hook] twice); bptr, back post treble (yarn round hook, take hook from back to front, around post of next st then to back again, yarn round hook and pull through, [yarn round hook and pull through first 2 loops on hook] twice); slst, slip st; chsp, chain space.

BLANKET

Main part: With 4.00 hook, make 84ch.

Foundation row (wrong side): 1tr in 4th ch from hook (counts as 2 sts), [1tr in next ch] to end – 82 sts.

1st row: 2ch (counts as 1htr), [1fptr in each of next 8 sts, 1bptr in each of next 8 sts] to last st, 1htr in last st, turn.

2nd to 5th rows: As 1st row.

6th row: 2ch (counts as 1htr), [1bptr in each of next 8 sts, 1fptr in each of next 8 sts] to last st, 1htr in last st, turn.

7th to 10th rows: As 6th row. These 10 rows form pattern.

Repeat these 10 rows, 5 times more, then work 1st to 5th rows again. Do not turn.

Edging: Change to 3.50 hook.

1st round: Work along side edge of blanket thus: 2ch (counts as 1dc and 1ch), miss first row-end, [1dc in next row-end, 1ch] to end, work along ch edge thus: 1dc in first st, [1ch, miss 1 st, 1dc in next st] to last st, 1ch, miss last st, work along other side edge of blanket thus: [1dc in next row-end, 1ch] to end, work along top edge thus: 1dc in first st, [1ch, miss 1 st, 1dc in next st] to last st, 1ch, miss last st, slst in first of 2ch.

2nd and 3rd rounds: Slst in first chsp, 2ch (counts as 1dc and 1ch), miss 1dc, [1dc in next chsp, 1ch, miss 1dc] to end, slst in first of 2ch. Fasten off.

BUMPER

With 4.00 hook, make 196ch.

Foundation row (wrong side): 1tr in 4th ch from hook (counts as 2 sts), [1tr in next ch] to end – 194 sts.

1st row: 2ch (counts as 1htr), [1fptr in each of next 8 sts, 1bptr in each of next 8 sts] to last st, 1htr in last st, turn.

2nd to 5th rows: As 1st row.

6th row: 2ch (counts as 1htr), [1bptr in each of next 8 sts, 1fptr in each of next 8 sts] to last st, 1htr in last st, turn.

7th to 10th rows: As 6th row. These 10 rows form pattern.

Repeat these 10 rows, once more, then work 1st to 5th rows again. Do not turn.

Edging: Change to 3.50 hook.

1st round: Work along side edge of bumper thus: 2ch (counts as 1dc and 1ch), miss first row-end, [1dc in next row-end, 1ch] to end, work along ch edge thus: 1dc in first st, [1ch, miss 1 st, 1dc in next st] to last st, 1ch, miss last st, work along other side edge of bumper thus: [1dc in next row-end, 1ch] to end, work along top edge thus: 1dc in first st, [1ch, miss 1 st, 1dc in next st] to last st, 1ch, miss last st, slst in first of 2ch.

2nd and 3rd rounds: Slst in first chsp, 2ch (counts as 1dc and 1ch), miss 1dc, [1dc in next chsp, 1ch, miss 1dc] to end, slst in first of 2ch. Fasten off.

Mark 4 tie positions on top edge of bumper: one at each end and one about 20cm from each end.

BUMPER TIES (MAKE 4)

With 4.00 hook, make 8ch.

Foundation row: 1dc in 4th ch from hook (counts as first chsp and 1dc), [1ch, miss 1ch, 1dc in next ch] twice, turn.

Pattern row: 2ch (counts as first chsp), miss first dc, [1dc in chsp, 1ch, miss 1dc] twice, 1dc in last chsp, turn.

Pattern another 30 rows.

Joining row: Place last row of tie at one marked position on top edge of bumper and work slst through every st on both layers, turn.

Next row: Work through both layers, 2ch (counts as first chsp), miss first st, [1dc in next st, 1ch, miss 1st] twice, 1dc in last chsp, turn.

Pattern another 31 rows. Fasten off.

Mandala Cushion

Our circle cushion will bring good vibes to your abode

DIFFICULTY

✕ ✕ ✕ ✕

WHAT YOU NEED

- 4mm crochet hook
- 33cm circular cushion pad
- Sirdar Hayfield Bonus DK (100% acrylic)

Colour 1: 1 x 100g (280m) Mustard (766)
Colour 2: 1 x 100g (280m) Blue (994)
Colour 3: 1 x 100g (280m) Teal (829)
Colour 4: 1 x 100g (280m) Purple (840)

MEASUREMENTS

Approximately 33cm/13in diameter, to fit a

33cm/13in round cushion pad.

ABBREVIATIONS

Ch, chain; st(s), stitch(es); yrh, yarn round hook; tr, treble crochet; slst, slip stitch; sp(s), space(s); dc, double crochet; htr, half treble crochet; dtr, double treble crochet.

FRONT

1st round: With 4mm hook and Purple, make a slip ring as follows: wind yarn round index finger of left hand to form a ring, insert hook into ring, yrh and pull through, 3ch (counts as 1tr), work 17tr in ring, slst in 3rd of beginning 3ch, pull end of yarn tightly to close ring. Fasten off – 18 sts.

2nd round: Join Teal with a slst to any sp between 2 tr, 1ch (does not count as a st), 1dc in same sp, [1dc in sp between next 2 tr] to end, slst in first dc. Fasten off.

3rd round: Join Mustard with a slst to any dc, 5ch (counts as 1tr and 2ch), 1tr in same st at base of 5ch, [skip next st, (1tr, 2ch, 1tr) in next st] to end, slst in 3rd of beginning 5ch. Fasten off – 9 groups of (1tr, 2ch, 1tr).

4th round: Join Denim with a slst to any sp between 2 tr (and not into the 2ch sp), 5ch (counts as 1tr and 2ch), 1tr in same sp at base of 5ch, *1ch, skip next (1tr, 2ch, 1tr), work (1tr, 2ch, 1tr) in sp between next 2tr; repeat from * to end, slst in 3rd of beginning 5ch. Fasten off – 9 groups of (1tr, 2ch, 1tr) and 9 1ch sps.

5th round: Join Purple with a slst to any 1ch sp, 3ch (counts as 1tr), 2tr in same sp, 3tr in next 2ch sp, [3tr in next 1ch sp, 3tr in next 2ch sp] to end, slst in 3rd of beginning 3ch. Fasten off – 54 sts.

6th round: Join Teal with a slst to any 2nd tr of any 3tr group, 5ch (counts as 1tr and 2ch), 1tr in same st at base of 5ch, skip 1 st, [(1tr, 2ch, 1tr) in next st, skip 1 st] to end, slst in 3rd of beginning 5ch. Fasten off – 27 groups of (1tr, 2ch, 1tr).

7th round: Join Denim with a slst to any 2ch sp, 1ch (does not count as a st), 1dc in same 2ch sp, 1dc in each of next 2 tr, [1dc in next 2ch space, 1dc in each of next 2 tr] to end, slst in first dc. Fasten off – 81 sts.

8th round: Join Mustard with a slst to any dc in line with the 2ch sp from 6th round, 4ch (counts as 1tr and 1ch), [skip next st, 1tr in next st] to end,

slst in 3rd of beginning 4ch. Fasten off – 41 tr and 41 1ch sps.

9th round: Join Purple with a slst to any 1ch sp, 3ch (counts as 1tr), 1tr in same sp at base of 3ch, [2tr in next 1ch sp] to end, slst in 3rd of beginning 3ch. Fasten off – 82 sts.

10th round: Join Denim with a slst to any sp between any 2tr group, 1ch (does not count as a st), 1dc in same sp, [1dc in space between next 2 tr] to end, slst to first dc. Fasten off.

11th round: Join Teal with a slst to any dc, 5ch (counts as 1tr and 2ch), 1tr in same dc at base of 5ch, [1ch, skip next 2 sts, (1tr, ch2, 1tr) in next st] to end, 1ch, slst in 3rd of beginning 5ch. Fasten off – 28 groups of (1tr, 2ch, 1tr) and 28 1ch sps.

12th round: Join Mustard with a slst to any 1ch sp, ch4 (counts as 1dtr), 3dtr in next 2ch sp, [1dtr in next 1ch sp, 3dtr in next 2ch sp] to end, slst to 4th of beginning 4ch. Fasten off – 112 sts.

13th round: Join Purple with a slst to any dtr, 1ch (does not count as a st), 1dc in same st, [1dc in next st] to end, slst to first dc. Do not fasten off.

14th round: 1ch (does not count as a st), 1dc in same st, 1dc in each of next 2 sts, 2dc in next st, [1dc in each of next 3 sts, 2dc in next st] to end, slst to first dc. Fasten off – 140 sts.

15th round: Join Denim with a slst to any dc, 3ch (counts as 1tr), 1tr in same st at base of 3ch, 1ch, skip 1 st, [2tr in next st, 1ch, skip 1 st] to end, slst in 3rd of beginning 3ch. Fasten off – 70 groups of 2tr and 70 1ch sps.

16th round: Join Purple with a slst to any 1ch sp, 6ch (counts as 1tr and 3ch), 1tr in same sp, 1ch, skip next (2tr, 1ch, 2tr), [1tr in next 1ch sp, 3ch, 1tr in same sp, 1ch, skip next (2tr, 1ch, 2tr)] to end, slst to 3rd of beginning 6ch. Fasten off – 35 groups of (1tr, 3ch, 1tr) and 35 1ch sps.

17th round: Join Teal with a slst to any 3ch sp, 3ch (counts as 1tr), 2tr in same 3ch sp, 3tr in next 1ch space, [3tr in next 3ch space, 3tr in next 1ch sp] to end, slst in 3rd of beginning 3ch. Fasten off – 210 sts.

18th round: Join Mustard with a slst to any tr, ch4 (counts as 1tr and 1ch), skip next st, [1tr in next st, 1ch, skip next st] to end, slst in 4th of beginning 4ch. Fasten off – 105 tr and 105 1ch sps.

19th round: Join Denim with a slst to any 1ch space, ch4 (counts as 1dtr), 1dtr in same sp, [2dtr in next 1ch sp] to end, slst in 4th of beginning 4ch. Fasten off – 210 sts.

20th round: Join Purple with a slst to any dtr, ch3 (counts as 1tr), [1tr in next st] to end, slst in 3rd of beginning 3ch. Fasten off. Weave in ends.

BACK

1st round: With 4mm hook and Teal, make a slip ring as follows: wind yarn round index finger of left hand to form a ring, insert hook into ring, yrh and pull through, 1ch (does not count as a st), work 6dc in ring, slst in beginning 1ch, pull end of yarn tightly to close ring – 6 sts.

Continue to work in a spiral, without joining each round.

2nd round: [2dc in next st] 6 times –12 sts.

3rd round: [2dc in next st, 1dc in next st] 6 times – 18 sts.

4th round: [2dc in next st, 1dc in each of next 2 sts] 6 times – 24 sts.

5th round: 1dc in each of next 2 sts, [2dc in next st, 1dc in each of next 3 sts] 5 times, 2dc in next st, 1dc in next st –30 sts.

6th round: [2dc in next st, 1dc in each of next 4 sts] 6 times – 36 sts.

7th round: 1dc in each of next 3 sts, [2dc in next st, 1dc in each of next 5 sts] 5 times, 2dc in next st, 1dc in each of next 2 sts – 42 sts.

8th round: [2dc in next st, 1dc in each of next 6 sts] 6 times – 48 sts.

9th round: 1dc in each of next 4 sts, [2dc in next st, 1dc in each of next 7 sts] 5 times, 2dc in next st, 1dc in each of next 3 sts – 54 sts.

10th round: [2dc in next st, 1dc in each of next 8 sts6 times – 60 sts.

11th round: 1dc in each of next 5 sts, [2dc in next st, 1dc in each of next 9 sts] 5 times, 2dc in next st, 1dc in each of next 4 sts – 66 sts.

12th round: [2dc in next st, 1dc in each of next 10 sts] to end – 72 sts.

13th round: 1dc in each of next 6 sts, [2dc in next st, 1dc in each of next 11 sts] 5 times, 2dc in next st, 1 dc in each of next 5 sts – 78 sts.

14th to 44th rounds: Continue increasing in the pattern as set, increasing in first st of following round and every alternate (even numbered) round, and offsetting the increasing on following 2nd round and every alternate (odd numbered) round. Remember to work 1 more dc between the increases on every round and to work 1 more dc at the beginning of every odd numbered round – 264 sts.

45th round: 1dc in each of next 22 sts, [2dc in next st, 1dc in each of next 43 sts] 5 times, 2dc in next st, 1dc in each of next 21 sts – 270 sts.
Fasten off.

TO MAKE UP

The back and front have a different amount of stitches, therefore the back sts will be decreased evenly when joining the pieces. Insert cushion pad when two-thirds of the seam is joined.

Join back and front as follows: With wrong sides together and right sides facing out and with front piece on top, join Purple with a slst through any tr of front and any dc of back, ch1 (counts as 1dc), 1dc in next corresponding tr and dc, *insert hook through next corresponding tr and dc, yrh and pull loop through back dc only (and thus leaving 1 loop and front tr on hook), insert hook in next dc on back, yrh and pull through back dc, yrh and pull through all loops on hook to complete the decrease*, 1dc in each of next 3 corresponding tr and dc, repeat from * to * to decrease 1 st on back, [1dc in each of next 2 corresponding tr and dc, repeat from * to * to decrease 1 st on back, 1dc in each of next 3 corresponding tr and dc, repeat from * to * to decrease 1 st on back] 29 times, slst in first ch and continue with edging – 210 sts.

Edging: 1ch (counts as first dc), 1htr in next st, 3tr in next st, 1htr in next st, 1dc in next st, [1dc in next st, 1htr in next st, 3tr in next st, 1htr in next st, 1dc in next st] to end, slst in first ch – 294 sts.
Fasten off.

PATTERN NOTES

• Yarn amounts are based on average requirements and are therefore approximate. Instructions in square brackets are worked as stated after 2nd bracket.

Petals are started with a slip stitch into the centre of the flower and are built up until the head is bursting with them

Fresh As A Daisy

Dainty daisy motifs, in two different sizes, to put together in a multitude of ways to update your home or wardrobe

DIFFICULTY

✕ ✕ ✕ ✕

WHAT YOU NEED

· 3mm crochet hook
· Sewing needle
· Green, blue, purple, white, yellow and red stitch markers
· White and yellow sewing thread
· 1m of 1.5cm wide yellow ribbon
· Tote bag and t-shirt
· DMC Natura Just Cotton (100% cotton)

Place mat and coaster:
Colour 1: 1 x 50g (155m) White (N01)

Colour 2: 1 x 50g (155m) Yellow (N16)

Table runner:
Colour 1: 2 x 50g (155m) White (N01)
Colour 2: 1 x 50g (155m) Yellow (N16)

Bunting:
Colour 1: 1 x 50g (155m) White (N01)
Colour 2: 1 x 50g (155m) Yellow (N16)

Tote bag appliqué:
Colour 1: 1 x 50g (155m) White (N01)
Colour 2: 1 x 50g (155m) Yellow (N16)

MEASUREMENTS

Place mat: Approximately 23 x 33cm/9 x 13in.
Coaster: 11cm/4¼in diameter.

Table runner: Approximately 18 x 68cm/7 x 26¾in.
Bunting: 100m/39¼in long.

TENSION

Large daisy measures 12cm in diameter and small daisy measures 8cm in diameter, using 3mm hook.

ABBREVIATIONS

Ch, chain; st(s), stitch(es); dc, double crochet; dc2tog, double crochet 2 sts together (to decrease 1 st) thus: [insert hook into next st, yarn round hook, and pull a loop through] twice, yarn round hook and pull through all 3 loops on hook; slst, slip st.

LARGE DAISY

Centre: 1st round: With 3mm hook and Yellow, make a slip ring as follows: wind yarn round index finger of left hand to form a ring, insert hook into ring, yarn round hook and pull through, 1ch (does not count as a st), work 6dc in ring, pull end of yarn tightly to close ring – 6 sts.

2nd round: [2dc in next st] 6 times – 12 sts.

3rd round: [2dc in next st, 1dc in next st] 6 times – 18 sts.

4th round: [2dc in next st, 1dc in each of next 2 sts] 6 times – 24 sts. Slst to first dc. Fasten off.

Petal: Join White to any dc on last round of centre.

1st row: 1ch (does not count as a st throughout), slst in same place as join, 1dc in next st, turn – 2 sts.

2nd row: 1ch, 1dc in first st, 1dc in slst, turn.

3rd row: 1ch, 2dc in each st, turn – 4 sts.

4th row: 1ch, [1dc in next st] to end, turn.

5th row: 1ch, 2dc in first st, 1dc in each of next 2 sts, 2dc in last st, turn – 6 sts.

6th to 10th rows: As 4th row.

11th row: 1ch, dc2tog, 1dc in each of next 2 sts, dc2tog, turn – 4 sts.

12th row: As 4th row.

13th row: 1ch, [dc2tog] twice, turn – 2 sts.

14th row: 1ch, dc2tog – 1 st.

Fasten off.

With right side facing, rejoin White to next dc after previous petal on last round of centre and work 1st to 14th rows of petal.

Continue in this way, making petals around centre until 12 petals in total have been made.

SMALL DAISY

Centre: 1st round: With 3mm hook and Yellow, work as given for 1st round of large daisy – 6 sts.

2nd round: [2dc in next st] 6 times – 12 sts. Slst to first dc. Fasten off.

Petal: Join White to any dc on last round of centre.

1st row: 1ch (does not count as a st throughout), slst in same place as join, turn – 1 st.

2nd row: 1ch, 2dc in slst, turn – 2 sts.

3rd row: 1ch, 2dc in first st, 1dc in last st, turn – 3 sts.

4th and 5th rows: 1ch, [1dc in next st] to end, turn.

6th row: 1ch, dc2tog, 1dc in last st, turn – 2 sts.

7th row: 1ch, dc2tog – 1 st.

Fasten off.

With right side facing, rejoin White to next dc after previous petal on last round of centre and work 1st to 7th rows of petal.

Continue in this way, making petals around the centre until 12 petals in total have been made.

*Be unique and appliqué
on as many or as few motifs
as you please*

TABLE RUNNER

Make 8 large daisies and 8 small daisies.

Mark daisy petal points as follows:

On 6 large daisies, place blue marker on 1st point, purple marker on 4th point, green marker on 6th point and red marker on 11th point. On remaining 2 large daisies, place blue marker on 1st point, green marker on 3rd point and red marker on 11th point.

On 6 small daisies, place green marker on 1st point and place red marker on 6th point. On remaining 2 small daisies, place green marker on 1st point and red marker on 4th point.

Lay large daisies flat in a zigzag pattern, joining matching marked points together. Arrange small daisies between large daisies and join matching marked points together.

PLACE MAT

Make 3 large daisies and 6 small daisies. Mark petal points on daisies as follows:

For centre strip: On one large daisy for middle flower, place blue markers on 1st and 7th points and green markers on 4th and 10th points. On each of 2 remaining large daisies, place blue marker on 1st point and red marker on 3rd and 11th points.

For first side strip: On one small daisy for middle flower, place blue markers on 1st and 7th points and green markers on 4th point. On second small daisy, place blue marker on 1st point and red marker on 6th point, and on third small daisy place red marker on 8th point.

For second side strip: Mark 3 remaining small daisies to match first side strip, but on middle flower place green marker on 10th point instead of 4th point.

Lay 3 large daisies flat in horizontal line, with middle flower in centre and join by sewing, matching marked points together.

Arrange and join 3 small daisies in same way for each side strip. Place side strips on each side of large daisies strip and join matching marked points.

COASTER

Make 1 large daisy. Flatten daisy and sew overlapped petals in position.

BUNTING

Make 15 small daisies. Arrange 12 of the small daises into four triangles of 3 daisies each and join by sewing together where petal points touch. Beginning and ending about 15cm from ends of ribbon and spacing them evenly, place each triangle along ribbon, with a single daisy in between the triangles. Sew in position.

APPLIQUÉ

Make 2 large daisies and 1 small daisy. Flatten each daisy so that every alternate petal is on top and secure in position. Using the photo as a guide, arrange flowers on bag and sew around each centre, then catch petals halfway up.

PATTERN NOTES

- Yarn amounts are based on average requirements and are therefore approximate. Instructions in square brackets are worked as stated after 2nd bracket.

PATTERN NOTES

• Yarn amounts are based on average
  requirements and are therefore
  approximate. Instructions in square
  brackets are worked as stated after
  2nd bracket.

Coaster & Placemat

Brighten up and protect your table

DIFFICULTY

✕ ✕ ✕ ✕

WHAT YOU NEED

- 3.00 crochet hook
- Patons 100% Cotton 4 Ply
- Colour 1: 1 x 100g (330m) Red (1115)
- Colour 2: 2 x 100g (330m) Cream (1692)

MEASUREMENTS

Coaster: Approx 12cm x 12cm/4¾ x 4¾in.

Placemat: Approx 31cm x 36cm/12 x 14in.

ABBREVIATIONS

Ch, chain; st, stitch; dc, double crochet; tr, treble; htr, half treble; yoh, yarn over hook; tr2cl, 2tr cluster (yoh, insert hook into 3rd ch from hook, yoh and pull through, yoh and pull through 2 loops on hook, yoh, insert hook into same ch as before, yoh and pull through, yoh and pull through 2 loops on hook, yoh and pull through all 3 loops on hook); spike, (insert hook into next tr, yoh and pull through, insert hook into base of same tr 1 row below, yoh and pull long loop through, insert hook into top of same tr as at beginning, yoh and pull through all 3 loops on hook); dbl spike, double spike (insert hook into next tr, yoh and pull through, insert hook at base of tr 1 row below and 2 sts forward, yoh and pull long loop through, insert hook at base of tr 1 row below and 2 sts backwards, yoh and pull long loop through, insert hook into top of same tr as at beginning, yoh and pull through all 4 loops on hook); fwd spike, forward spike (insert hook into next tr, yoh and pull through, insert hook at base of tr 1 row below and 2 sts forward, yoh and pull long loop through, insert hook in top of same tr as at beginning, yoh and pull through all 3 loops on hook); bkd spike, backward spike (insert hook into next tr, yoh and pull through, insert hook at base of tr 1 row below and 2 sts backwards, yoh and pull long loop through, insert hook in top of same tr as at beginning, yoh and pull through all 3 loops on hook); slst, slip st; tr3tog, work 3tr together thus: [yoh, insert hook in next st, yoh and pull through, yoh and pull through 2 loops on hook] 3 times, yoh and pull through all 4 loops on hook).

COASTER

1st round: With 3.00 hook and Red, make a slip ring as follows: wind yarn round index finger of left hand to form a ring, insert hook into ring, yarn over hook and pull through, 1ch (does not count as a st throughout), 12dc in ring, slst in first dc, pull end of yarn tightly to close ring – 12dc.

2nd round: 1ch 1dc in base of ch, 3dc in next dc for corner, [1dc in each of next 2dc, 3dc in next dc for corner] 3 times, 1dc into last dc, slst in first dc – 20dc.

3rd round: Slst in next dc, 3ch (counts as 1tr throughout), 1tr in same place as previous slst, work 1tr, 1ch, 1tr, 1ch and 1tr all in corner dc,* [miss next dc, 1tr in next dc, 1tr in missed dc] twice, work 1tr, 1ch, 1tr, 1ch and 1tr all in corner dc, repeat from * twice more, miss next dc, 1tr in last dc, 1tr in missed dc, slst in 3rd of 3ch – 28tr.

4th round: 1ch, 1dc in base of ch, 1dc in each of next 2tr, 1dc in next ch, 3dc in corner tr, [1dc in next ch, 1dc in each of next 6tr, 1dc in next ch, 3dc in corner tr] 3 times, 1dc in next ch, 1dc in each of last 3tr, slst in first dc – 44dc.

5th round: Slst in each of next 3dc and close up, 3ch, 1tr in previous slst, miss next dc, 1tr in next dc, 1tr in missed dc, work 1tr, 1ch, 1tr, 1ch and 1tr all in corner dc, * [miss next dc, 1tr in next dc, 1tr in missed dc] 5 times, work 1tr, 1ch, 1tr, 1ch and 1tr all in corner dc, repeat from * twice more, [miss next dc, 1tr in next dc, 1tr in missed dc] 3 times, slst in 3rd of 3ch – 52tr.

6th round: 1ch, 1dc in base of ch, 1dc in each of next 4tr, 1dc in next ch, 3dc in corner tr, [1dc in next ch, 1dc in each of next 12tr, 1dc in next ch, 3dc in corner tr] 3 times, 1dc in next ch, 1dc in each of last 7tr, slst in first dc – 68dc.

7th round: 3ch, 1tr in previous dc, [miss next dc, 1tr in next dc, 1tr in missed dc] 3 times, work 1tr, 1ch, 1tr, 1ch and 1tr all in corner dc, * [miss next dc, 1tr in next dc, 1tr in missed dc] 8 times, work 1tr, 1ch, 1tr, 1ch and 1tr all in corner dc, repeat from * twice more, [miss next dc, 1tr in next dc, 1tr in missed dc] 4 times, slst in 3rd of 3ch – 76tr.

8th round: 1ch, 1dc in base of ch, 1dc in each of next 8tr, 1dc in next ch, 3dc in corner tr, [1dc in next ch, 1dc in each of next 18tr, 1dc in next ch, 3dc in corner tr] 3 times, 1dc in next ch, 1dc in each of last 9tr, slst in first dc – 92dc. Break off Red. Join in Cream.

9th round: 1ch, 1dc in base of ch, 1dc in each of next 10dc, 3dc in corner dc, [1dc in each of next 22dc, 3dc in corner dc] 3 times, 1dc in each of last 11dc, slst in first dc – 100dc.

10th round: Slst in next dc, 5ch, tr2cl in 3rd ch from hook, [miss next 2dc, 1htr in next dc, 3ch, tr2cl in 3rd ch from hook] twice, miss next 2dc, 1htr in each of next 2dc, 3ch, tr2cl in 3rd ch from hook, miss corner dc, 1htr in each of next 2dc, * [3ch, tr2cl in 3rd ch from hook, miss next 2dc, 1htr next dc]

7 times, 1htr in next dc, 3ch, tr2cl in 3rd ch from hook, miss corner dc, 1htr in each of next 2dc, repeat from * twice more, [3ch, tr2cl in 3rd ch from hook, miss next 2dc, 1htr in next dc] 3 times, 3ch, tr2cl in 3rd ch from hook, slst into 2nd of 5ch.

11th round: 5ch (counts as 1htr and 3ch), 1htr in next htr, 3ch, 1htr in next htr, 3ch, miss next htr, 1htr in next htr, 7ch, miss next htr, 1htr in next htr,* [3ch, 1htr in next htr] 6 times, 3ch, miss next htr, 1htr in next htr, 7ch, miss next htr, 1htr in in next htr, repeat from * twice, [3ch, 1htr in next htr] 3 times, 3ch, slst in 2nd of 5ch.

Fasten off.

Neaten ends. Press and pull into square shape.

PLACEMAT

With 3.00 hook and Red, make 13ch.

1st round: 2dc into 2nd ch from hook, 1dc in each of next 10ch, 3dc in last ch, work along other side of chain thus: 1dc in each of next 10ch, 1dc in base of 2dc at beginning, slst in first dc – 26dc.

2nd round: 1ch (does not count as a st throughout), 1dc in base of ch, 3dc in next dc for corner, 1dc in each of next 10dc, 3dc in next dc for corner, 1dc in next dc, 3dc in next dc for corner, 1dc in each of next 10dc, 3dc in next dc for corner, slst in first dc – 34dc.

3rd round: 1ch, 1dc in base of ch, 1dc in next dc, 3dc in corner dc, 1dc in each of next 12dc, 3dc in corner dc, 1dc in each of next 3dc, 3dc in corner dc, 1dc in each of next 12dc, 3dc in corner dc, 1dc in last dc, slst in top of first dc – 42dc.

4th round: 3ch (counts as 1tr throughout), miss next dc, 1tr in next dc, 1tr in missed dc, * work 1tr, 1ch, 1tr, 1ch and 1tr all in corner dc, [miss next dc, 1tr in next dc, 1tr in missed dc] 7 times, work 1tr, 1ch, 1tr, 1ch and 1tr all in corner dc, miss next dc, 1tr in next dc, 1tr in missed dc *, 1tr in next dc, miss next dc, 1tr in next dc, 1tr in missed dc, work from * to * once, slst in 3rd of 3ch – 58 sts.

5th round: 1ch, 1dc in base of ch, 1dc in each of next 3tr, 1dc in next ch, 3dc in corner tr, * 1dc in next ch, 1dc in each of next 16tr, 1dc in next ch, 3dc in corner tr, 1dc in next ch *, 1dc in each of next 7tr, 1dc in next ch, 3dc in corner tr, work from * to * once, 1dc in each of last 3tr, slst in top of first dc – 66 sts.

6th round: 3ch, 1tr in next tr, * [miss next dc, 1tr in next dc, 1tr in missed dc] twice, work 1tr, 1ch, 1tr, 1ch and 1tr all in corner dc, [miss next dc, 1tr in next dc, 1tr in missed dc] 10 times, work 1tr, 1ch, 1tr, 1ch and 1tr all in corner dc, [miss next dc, 1tr in next dc, 1tr in missed dc] twice *, tr3tog, work from * to * once, 1tr in last dc, slst in 3rd of 3ch – 80 sts.

7th round: 1ch, 1dc in base of ch, 1dc in each of next 6tr, * 1dc in next ch, 3dc in corner tr, 1dc in next ch, 1dc in each of next 22tr, 1dc in next ch, 3dc in corner tr, 1dc in next ch *, 1dc in each of next 5tr, 3dc in next sts, 1dc in each of next 5tr, work from * to * once, 1dc in each of last 6tr, slst in top of first dc – 90 sts.

8th round: 3ch, * [miss next dc, 1tr in next dc, 1tr in missed dc] 4 times, work 1tr, 1ch, 1tr, 1ch and 1tr all in corner dc, [miss next dc, 1tr in next dc, 1tr in missed dc] 13 times, work 1tr, 1ch, 1tr, 1ch and 1tr all in corner dc, [miss next dc, 1tr in next dc, 1tr in missed dc] 4 times *, 1tr in next dc, work from * to * once, slst in 3rd of 3ch – 106 sts.

9th round: 1ch, 1dc in base of ch, 1dc in each of next 9tr, * 1dc in next ch, 3dc in corner tr, 1dc in next ch, 1dc in each of next 28tr, 1dc in next ch, 3dc in corner tr, 1dc in next ch *, 1dc in each of next 19tr, work from * to * once, 1dc in each of last 9tr, slst in top of first dc – 114dc. Join in Cream.

10th round: 1ch, 1dc in base of ch, * [1dc in next dc] to corner dc, 3dc in corner dc, work from * 3 times more, [1dc in next dc] to end, slst in top of first dc.

11th round: 3ch, * [1tr in next dc] to corner dc, 5tr in corner dc, work from * 3 times more, [1tr in next dc] to end, slst in 3rd of 3ch. Break off Cream. Change to Red.

12th round: 1ch, dbl spike in first st, 1dc in each of next 3tr, [dbl spike, 1dc each of next 3tr] twice, bkd spike, * 1dc in each of next 2tr, work 1dc, spike and 1dc in corner tr, 1dc in each of next 2tr, fwd spike, [1dc in each of next 3tr, dbl spike] 3 times, 1dc in each of next 3tr, bkd spike, fwd spike, [1dc in each of next 3tr, dbl spike] 3 times, 1dc in each of next 3tr, bkd spike, 1dc in each of next 2tr, work 1dc, spike and 1dc in corner tr, 1dc in each of next 2tr, fwd spike *, [1dc in each of next 3tr, dbl spike] 5 times, 1dc in each of next 3tr, bkd spike, work from * to * once, [1dc in each of next 3tr, dbl spike] twice, 1dc in each of last 3tr, slst in first st – 146sts.

13th round: 1ch, 1dc in base of ch, * [1dc in next st] to corner st, 3dc in corner st, work from * 3 times more, [1dc in next st] to end, slst in top of first dc.

14th round: 3ch, * [miss next dc, 1tr in next dc, 1tr in missed dc] 8 times, work 1tr, 1ch, 1tr, 1ch and 1tr all in corner dc, [miss next dc, 1tr in next dc, 1tr in missed dc] 21 times, work 1tr, 1ch, 1tr, 1ch and 1tr in corner dc, [miss next dc, 1tr in next dc, 1tr in missed dc] 8 times *, 1tr in next st, work from * to * once, slst in 3rd of 3ch – 170 sts.

15th round: 1ch, 1dc in base of ch, * [1dc in next tr] to 1ch before corner tr, 1dc in next ch, 3dc in corner tr, 1dc in next ch, work, from * 3 times more, [1dc in next tr] to end, slst in top of first dc.

16th round: 3ch, 1tr in next dc, * [miss next dc, 1tr in next dc, 1tr in missed dc] 9 times, work 1tr, 1ch, 1tr, 1ch and 1tr in corner dc, [miss next dc, 1tr in next dc, 1tr in missed dc] 24 times, work 1tr, 1ch, 1tr, 1ch and 1tr all in corner dc, [miss next dc, 1tr in next dc, 1tr in missed dc] 9 times *, tr3tog, work from * to * once, 1tr in last dc, slst in 3rd of 3ch – 192 sts.

17th round: 1ch, 1dc in base of ch,* [1dc in next tr] to 1ch before corner tr, 1dc in next ch, 3dc in corner st, 1dc in next ch *, work from * to * once, 1dc in each of next 19tr, 3dc in next st, work from * to * twice, [1dc in next tr] to end, slst in top of first dc – 202dc.

18th round: 3ch,* [miss next dc, 1tr in next dc, 1tr in missed dc] 11 times, work 1tr, 1ch, 1tr, 1ch and 1tr all in corner dc, [miss next dc, 1tr in next dc, 1tr in missed dc] 27 times, work 1tr, 1ch, 1tr, 1ch and 1tr all in corner dc, [miss next dc, 1tr next dc, 1tr in missed dc] 11 times *, 1tr in next dc, work from * to * once, slst in 3rd of 3ch – 218 sts.

19th round: 1ch, 1dc in base of ch, * [1dc in next tr] to 1ch before corner tr, 1dc in next ch, 3dc in corner tr, 1dc in next ch, work from * 3 times more, [1dc in next tr] to end, slst in top of first dc.

Join in Cream.

20th and 21st rounds: Work 10th and 11th rounds. Break off Cream. Change to Red.

22nd round: 1ch, dbl spike in first st, [1dc in each of next 3tr, dbl spike]

6 times, * 1dc in each of next 4tr, work 1dc, spike and 1dc all in corner tr, 1dc in each of next 4tr, [dbl spike, 1dc in each of next 3tr] 7 times, bkd spike, fwd spike, [1dc in each of next 3tr, dbl spike] 7 times, 1dc in each of next 4tr, work 1dc, spike and 1dc in corner tr, 1dc in each of next 4tr *, [dbl spike, 1dc in each of next 3tr] 12 times, dbl spike, work from * to * once, [dbl spike, 1dc in each of next 3tr] 6 times, slst in first st – 258 sts.

23rd round: As 13th round.

24th round: 3ch, * [miss next dc, 1tr in next dc, 1tr in missed dc] 15 times, work 1tr, 1ch, 1tr, 1ch and 1tr all in corner dc, [miss next dc, 1tr in next dc, 1tr in missed dc] 35 times, work 1tr, 1ch, 1tr, 1ch and 1tr all in corner dc, [miss next dc, 1tr in next dc, 1tr in missed dc] 15 times *, 1tr in next dc, work from * to * once, slst in 3rd of 3ch – 282 sts.

25th round: As 15th round.

26th round: 3ch, 1tr in next dc, * [miss next dc, 1tr in next dc, 1tr in missed dc] 16 times, work 1tr, 1ch, 1tr, 1ch and 1tr all in corner dc, [miss next dc, 1tr in next dc, 1tr in missed dc] 38 times, work 1tr, 1ch, 1tr, 1ch and 1tr all in corner dc, [miss next dc, 1tr in next dc, 1tr in missed dc] 16 times *, tr3tog, work from * to * once, 1tr in last dc, slst in 3rd of 3ch – 304 sts.

27th round: 1ch, 1dc in base of ch, * [1dc in next tr] to 1ch before corner tr, 1dc in next ch, 3dc in corner tr, 1dc in next ch *, work from * to * once, 1dc in each of next 33tr, 3dc in next st, work from * to * twice, [1dc in next tr] to end, slst in top of first dc – 314dc.

28th round: 3ch, * [miss next dc, 1tr in next dc, 1tr in missed dc] 18 times,

work 1tr, 1ch, 1tr, 1ch and 1tr all in corner dc, [miss next dc, 1tr in next dc, 1tr in missed dc] 41 times, work 1tr, 1ch, 1tr, 1ch and 1tr all in corner dc, [miss next dc, 1tr in next dc, 1tr in missed dc] 18 times *, 1tr in next dc, work from * to * once, slst in 3rd of 3ch – 330 sts.

29th round: As 15th round.

Break off Red. Join in Cream.

30th round: As 10th round.

31st round: 5ch, tr2cl in 3rd ch from hook, miss next 2dc, 1htr in next dc, [3ch, tr2cl in 3rd ch from hook, miss next 2dc, 1htr in next dc] 12 times, 1htr in next dc, 3ch, tr2cl in 3rd ch from hook, miss corner dc, 1htr in each of next 2dc, * [3ch, tr2cl in 3rd ch from hook, miss next 2dc, 1htr in next dc] 29 times, 1htr in next dc, 3ch, tr2cl in 3rd ch from hook, miss corner st, 1htr in each of next 2dc *, [3ch, tr2cl in 3rd ch from hook, miss next 2dc, 1htr in next dc] 26 times, 1htr in next dc, 3ch, tr2cl in 3rd ch from hook, miss corner dc, 1htr in each of next 2dc, work from * to * once, [3ch, tr2cl in 3rd ch from hook, miss next 2dc, 1htr in next dc] 12 times, 3ch, tr2cl in 3rd ch from hook, slst in 2nd of 5ch.

32nd round: 5ch (counts as 1htr and 3ch), 1htr in next htr, * [3ch, 1htr in next htr] to 2 to htr before corner, miss next htr, 1htr in next htr, 7ch, miss next htr, 1htr in next htr, work from * 3 times more, [3ch, 1htr in next htr] to end, ending 3ch, slst in 2nd of 5ch. Fasten off.

Neaten ends. Press and pull into rectangular shape.

Windmill Blanket

This blanket design is cute and versatile

PATTERN NOTES

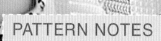

- Yarn amounts are based on average
requirements and are therefore
approximate. Instructions in square
brackets are worked as stated after
2nd bracket.

DIFFICULTY

✕ ✕ ✕ ✕

WHAT YOU NEED

• 5mm (No. 6) crochet hook
• DMC Natura Medium (100% cotton)

Colour 1: 9 x 50g (75m) White (01)
Colour 2: 2 x 50g (75m) Grey (12)
Colour 3: 2 x 50g (75m) Mint (137)
Colour 4: 2 x 50g (75m) Coral (444)

MEASUREMENTS

Approximately 70 x 100cm/27½ x 39½in.

ABBREVIATIONS

Ch, chain; st, stitch; dc, double crochet; slst, slip st;
yrh, yarn round hook.

MOTIF

First square: With 5mm hook and White, make 23ch.

1st row (right side): 1dc in 2nd ch from hook (counts as 1 st), 1dc in each of next 20ch, insert hook in last ch, yrh and pull through, join in Grey, yrh and pull through 2 loops on hook, turn – 22dc.

Twisting yarns together on wrong sides when changing colours and working last dc before colour change as follows: with yarn in use, insert hook in next dc, yrh and pull through, with next colour, yrh and pull through 2 loops on hook, continue thus:

2nd row: With Grey, 1ch (does not count as a st throughout), 1dc in first dc, with White, 1dc in each of last 21dc, turn.

3rd row: With White, 1ch, 1dc in each of first 20dc, with Grey, 1dc in each of last 2dc, turn.

4th row: With Grey, 1ch, 1dc in each of first 3dc, with White, 1dc in each of last 19dc, turn.

5th row: With White, 1ch, 1dc in each of first 18dc, with Grey, 1dc in each of last 4dc, turn.

6th row: With Grey, 1ch, 1dc in each of first 5dc, with White, 1dc in each of last 17dc, turn.

7th row: With White, 1ch, 1dc in each of first 16dc, with Grey, 1dc in each of last 6dc, turn.

8th row: With Grey, 1ch, 1dc in each of first 7dc, with White, 1dc in each of last 15dc, turn.

9th row: With White, 1ch, 1dc in each of first 14dc, with Grey, 1dc in each of last 8dc, turn.

10th row: With Grey, 1ch, 1dc in each of first 9dc, with White, 1dc in each of last 13dc, turn.

11th row: With White, 1ch, 1dc in each of first 12dc, with Grey, 1dc in each of last 10dc, turn.

12th row: With Grey, 1ch, 1dc in each of first 11dc, with White, 1dc in each of last 11dc, turn.

13th row: With White, 1ch, 1dc in each of first 10dc, with Grey, 1dc in each of last 12dc, turn.

14th row: With Grey, 1ch, 1dc in each of first 13dc, with White, 1dc in each of last 9dc, turn.

15th row: With White, 1ch, 1dc in each of first 8dc, with Grey, 1dc in each of last 14dc, turn.

16th row: With Grey, 1ch, 1dc in each of first 15dc, with White, 1dc in each of last 7dc, turn.

17th row: With White, 1ch, 1dc in each of first 6dc, with Grey, 1dc in each of last 16dc, turn.

18th row: With Grey, 1ch, 1dc in each of first 17dc, with White, 1dc in each of last 5dc, turn.

19th row: With White, 1ch, 1dc in each of first 4dc, with Grey, 1dc in each of last 18dc, turn.

20th row: With Grey, 1ch, 1dc in first 19dc, with White, 1dc in each of last 3dc, turn.

21st row: With White, 1ch, 1dc in each of first 2dc, with Grey, 1dc in each of last 20dc, turn.

22nd row: With Grey, 1ch, 1dc in first 21dc, with White, 1dc in last dc, turn.

23rd row: With Grey, 1ch, 1dc in each of 22dc. Fasten off.

Second square: With right side facing, using 5mm hook and White, work 22dc along row-ends of Grey section of first square, changing to Grey on last stage of last dc.

Work 2nd to 23rd rows as on first square.

Third square: With right side facing, using 5mm hook and White, work 22dc along row-ends of Grey section of second square, changing to Grey on last stage of last dc.

Work 2nd to 23rd rows as on first square.

Fourth square: With right side facing, using 5mm hook and White, work 22dc along row-ends of Grey section of third square, changing to Grey on last stage of last dc. Work 2nd to 23rd rows as on first square. Oversew Grey section of fourth square to White section on first square to complete first motif.

Edging: With right side facing, using 5mm hook, join White to any corner on motif, 1ch, 3dc in same corner as join, [43dc along side edge to next corner, 3dc in corner] 3 times, 43dc along final edge, slst in first dc – 184 sts. Work 1 round in dc, working 3dc in centre dc at each corner. Fasten off. Make another motif in colours as set.

Make 2 more motifs, using Coral instead of Grey.

Make 2 more motifs, using Mint instead of Grey.

TO MAKE UP

Arrange motifs in 3 rows of 2 motifs each. Working horizontally and with wrong sides together, join motifs using 5mm hook and White, by working slst below loops of each corresponding pair of stitches along fastened-off edge. Join motifs vertically in same way until the blanket is complete.

Border: With right side facing and using 5mm hook, join White to any corner on blanket, 1ch, 3dc in same corner as join, [1dc in each st to next corner, 3dc in corner] 3 times, 1dc in each st along final edge, slst in first dc. Work 3 rounds in dc, beginning each round with 1ch and working 3dc in centre dc at each corner on each round, ending each round with slst in first dc. Fasten off.

Tablet Case

Keep your tablet safe and looking great in this funky and easy-to-make case

DIFFICULTY

✕ ✕ ✕ ✕

WHAT YOU NEED

- 4mm crochet hook
- 1 button
- sewing needle and light grey sewing thread
- DMC Woolly (100% wool)
  Colour 1: 2 x 50 (125m) Light Grey (71)
  Colour 2: 1 x 50 (125m) Orange (10)

MEASUREMENTS

Approximately 19 x 26cm/7½ x 10¼in.

ABBREVIATIONS

Ch, chain; st, stitch; tr, treble; slst, slip stitch; yrh, yarn round hook; bptr, back post treble, (work a tr st around post of st in previous round thus: yrh, insert hook from back to front and around post of next st to back,yrh and pull loop through, yrh and pull through first 2 loops on hook, yrh and pull through last 2 loops on hook); fptr, front post treble, (work a tr st around post of st in previous round thus: yrh, insert hook from front to back and around post of next st to front, yrh and pull loop through, yrh and pull through first 2 loops on hook, yrh and pull through last 2 loops on hook).

TO MAKE

With 4mm hook and Orange, make 78ch, taking care not to twist ch, join with a slst in first ch.

Foundation round: 3ch (counts as 1tr throughout instructions), [1tr in next ch] 77 times, slst in top of 3ch – 78 sts.

1st round: 3ch, bptr around each of next 2 sts, [1tr in next st, bptr around each of next 2 sts] to end, slst around post of 3ch.

2nd round: 3ch, 1tr in each of next 2 sts, [fptr around next st, 1tr in eachof next 2 sts] to end, slst around post of 3ch. The last 2 rounds form the pattern.

Repeat 1st and 2nd rounds, 5 times more, then work 1st round again.

Break off Orange. Join in Light Grey.

Work 2nd round.

Repeat 1st and 2nd rounds, 10 times more.

Edging round: Slst in each of next 20 sts, for button loop make 25ch, slst in base of 25ch, [slst in next st] 57 times.

Fasten off and neaten ends.

Flatten the piece with button loop at centre and join seam of foundation round together. Sew on button to correspond with button loop

PATTERN NOTES

- Yarn amounts are based on average requirements and are therefore approximate. Instructions in square brackets are worked as stated after 2nd bracket.

Choose your favourite contrast shades

Gifts & Amigurumi

PATTERN NOTES

• Yarn amounts are based on average
requirements and are therefore
approximate. Instructions in square
brackets are worked as stated after
2nd bracket.

Animal Magic

These beasts aren't wild – they're too cuddly for words

DIFFICULTY

✂ ✂ ✂ ✂

WHAT YOU NEED

• 3.00 and 4.00 crochet hooks
• Length of Brown yarn for embroidery
• Washable toy stuffing
• King Cole Bamboo Cotton 4ply
  (52% cotton, 48% bamboo viscose)

Lion:
Colour: 1 x 100g (371m) Latte (1027)
Hippo:
Colour: 1 x 100g (371m) Pebble (1022)
Giraffe:
Colour: 1 x 100g (371m) Cream (1019)

MEASUREMENTS

Approximately 20cm/8in tall, excluding top head

features.

ABBREVIATIONS

Ch, chain; dc, double crochet; st, stitch; htr, half treble; tr, treble; slst, slip stitch; yrh, yarn round hook; dc2tog, [insert hook in next st, yrh and pull through] twice, yrh and pull through all 3 loops on hook; htr2tog, [yrh, insert hook in next st, yrh and pull through] twice, yrh and pull through all 5 loops on hook.

LION

LEGS AND BODY

First leg: 1st round: With 3.00 hook, make slip ring as follows: wind yarn round index finger of left hand to form ring, insert hook into ring, yrh and pull through, 2ch (counts as 1htr throughout), work 7htr in ring, slst in top of 2ch, pull end of yarn tightly to close ring – 8 sts.

2nd round: 2ch, 1htr in base of 2ch, [2htr in next st] to end, slst in top of 2ch – 16 sts.

3rd and 4th rounds: 2ch, [1htr in next st] to end, slst in top of 2ch. Fasten off.

Second leg: Work 1st to 4th rounds of first leg.

Place right sides of legs together, [insert hook from inside of leg in next st on second leg, then in corresponding st on first leg and work slst] 3 times, turn, work slst as before across same 3 sts.

Body: 5th (joining) round: With right side facing, 1ch (does not count as a st), 1htr in each of first 13 sts of second leg, yrh, insert hook in htr below slst on second leg, yrh, insert hook in corresponding htr on first leg, yrh and pull through all 5 loops on hook, 1htr in each of next 13 sts of first leg, slst in top of first htr – 27 sts.

6th round: 2ch, 1htr in base of 2ch, [2htr in next st] to end, slst in top of 2ch – 54 sts.

7th to 11th rounds: 2ch, [1htr in next st] to end, slst in top of 2ch.

12th round: 2ch, 1htr in each of next 3 sts, htr2tog, [1htr in each of next 4 sts, htr2tog] to end, slst in top of 2ch – 45 sts.

13th and 14th rounds: 2ch, [1htr in next st] to end, slst in top of 2ch.

15th round: 2ch, 1htr in each of next 2 sts, htr2tog, [1htr in each of next 3 sts, htr2tog] to end, slst in top of 2ch – 36 sts.

16th and 17th rounds: 2ch, [1htr in next st] to end, slst in top of 2ch.

18th round: 2ch, 1htr in next st, htr2tog, [1htr in each of next 2 sts, htr2tog] to end, slst in top of 2ch – 27 sts.

19th and 20th rounds: 2ch, [1htr in next st] to end, slst in top of 2ch.

21st round: 2ch, htr2tog, [1htr in next st, htr2tog] to end, slst in top of 2ch – 18 sts.

22nd and 23rd rounds: 2ch, [1htr in next st] to end, slst in top of 2ch. Stuff body.

24th round: 1ch (does not count as a st), miss first st, 1htr in next st, [htr2tog] to end – 9 sts. Fasten off.

Gather fastened-off edge, pull up tightly and secure.

HEAD

1st round: With 3.00 hook, make slip ring as on first leg, 2ch (counts as 1htr throughout), work 7htr in ring, slst in top of 2ch, pull end of yarn tightly to close ring – 8 sts.

2nd round: 2ch, 1htr in base of 2ch, [2htr in next st] to end, slst in top of 2ch – 16 sts.

3rd round: 2ch, 2htr in next st, [1htr in next st, 2htr in next st] to end, slst in top of 2ch – 24 sts.

4th round: 2ch, 1htr in next st, 2htr in next st, [1htr in each of next 2 sts, 2htr in next st] to end, slst in top of 2ch – 32 sts.

5th round: 2ch, 1htr in each of next 2 sts, 2htr in next st, [1htr in each of next 3 sts, 2htr in next st] to end, slst in top of 2ch – 40 sts.

6th to 8th rounds: 2ch, [1htr in next st] to end, slst in top of 2ch.

9th round: 2ch, 1htr in each of next 2 sts, htr2tog, [1htr in each of next 3 sts, htr2tog] to end, slst in top of 2ch – 32 sts.

10th and 11th rounds: 2ch, [1htr in next st] to end, slst in top of 2ch.

12th round: 2ch, 1htr in next st, htr2tog, [1htr in each of next 2 sts, htr2tog] to end – 24 sts.

13th and 14th rounds: 2ch, [1htr in next st] to end, slst in top of 2ch.

17th round: 2ch, htr2tog, [1htr in next st, htr2tog] to end, slst in top of 2ch – 16 sts. Stuff head.

16th round: 1ch (does not count as a st), miss first st, 1htr in next st, [htr2tog] to end, slst in first htr – 8 sts.
Fasten off for lower head.

Gather fastened-off edge, pull up tightly and secure. With joins of rounds at back, position 7th round of head to fastened-off edge of body and 14th round of head 6 rounds down from top of body front, then sew head in position.

With Brown, embroider eyes, tip of nose and mouth on front of head.

MANE

With 3.00 hook, make 48ch, slst in first ch, making sure that the ch is not twisted.

1st round: Miss first ch, [8tr in next ch, miss next ch, slst in next ch, miss next ch] 11 times, 8tr in next ch, miss next ch, slst in last ch. Fasten off.
Place ch edge around head and sew in position.

EARS (MAKE 2)

With 3.00 hook, make 2ch.

1st round: 6htr in 2nd ch from hook, slst in first htr.

2nd round: 2ch, 1htr in base of 2ch, [2htr in next st] 5 times, slst in top of 2ch – 12 sts. Fasten off.
Sew ears to top of head.

ARMS (MAKE 2)

1st round: With 3.00 hook, make slip ring as on first leg, 2ch (counts as 1htr throughout), work 7htr in ring, slst in top of 2ch, pull end of yarn tightly to close ring – 8 sts.

2nd round: 2ch, 1htr in base of 2ch, [2htr in next st] to end, slst in top of 2ch – 16 sts.

3rd and 4th rounds: 2ch, [1htr in next st] to end, slst in top of 2ch.

5th round: 2ch, [htr2tog, 1htr next st] to end, slst in top of 2ch – 11 sts.

6th to 8th rounds: 2ch, [1htr in next st] to end, slst in top of 2ch. Stuff arm.

9th round: 1ch (does not count as a st), miss first st, 1htr in next st, [htr2tog, 1htr next st] to end, slst in first htr – 7 sts.

10th round: 2ch, [1htr in next st] to end, slst in top of 2ch. Fasten off.
Flatten fastened-off edge and sew to sides of body.

TAIL

With 4.00 hook and using 6 strands of yarn together, make 3ch. Fasten off.
Sew one end of tail to back body. Trim other end for a tuft.

HIPPO
LEGS AND BODY

Work as given for lion.

HEAD

1st round: With 3.00 hook, make slip ring as on first leg of lion, 2ch (counts as 1htr throughout), work 7htr in ring, slst in top of 2ch, pull end of yarn tightly to close ring – 8 sts.

2nd round: 2ch, 1htr in base of 2ch, [2htr in next st] to end, slst in top of 2ch – 16 sts.

3rd round: 2ch, 2htr in next st, [1htr in next st, 2htr in next st] to end, slst in top of 2ch – 24 sts.

4th round: 2ch, 1htr in next st, 2htr in next st, [1htr in each of next 2 sts, 2htr in next st] to end, slst in top of 2ch – 32 sts.

5th round: 2ch, 1htr in each of next 2 sts, 2htr in next st, [1htr in each of next 3 sts, 2htr in next st] to end, slst in top of 2ch – 40 sts.

6th to 8th rounds: 2ch, [1htr in next st] to end, slst in top of 2ch.

9th round: 2ch, 1htr in each of next 2 sts, htr2tog, [1htr in each of next 3 sts, htr2tog] to end, slst in top of 2ch – 32 sts.

10th to 12th rounds: 2ch, [1htr in next st] to end, slst in top of 2ch.

13th round: 2ch, 1htr in next st, htr2tog, [1htr in each of next 2 sts, htr2tog] to end, slst in top of 2ch – 24 sts.

14th to 16th rounds: 2ch, [1htr in next st] to end, slst in top of 2ch.

17th round: 2ch, htr2tog, [1htr in next st, htr2tog] to end, slst in top of 2ch – 16 sts. Stuff head.

18th round: 1ch (does not count as a st), miss first st, 1htr in next st, [htr2tog] to end – 8 sts. Fasten off for top of head.

Gather fastened-off edge, pull up tightly and secure. With joins of rounds at back, position 12th round of head to fastened-off edge of body and 6th round of head 6 rounds down from top of body front, then sew head in position. With Brown, embroider eyes and nostrils.

EARS, ARMS & TAIL

Work as given for lion.

GIRAFFE
LEGS AND BODY

Work as given for lion.

HEAD

1st round: With 3.00 hook, make slip ring as on first leg of lion, 2ch (counts as 1htr throughout), work 7htr in ring, slst in top of 2ch, pull end of yarn tightly to close ring.

2nd round: 2ch, 1htr in base of 2ch, [2htr in next st] to end, slst in top of 2ch – 16 sts.

3rd round: 2ch, 2htr in next st, [1htr in next st, 2htr in next st] to end, slst in top of 2ch – 24 sts.

4th round: 2ch, 1htr in next st, 2htr in next st, [1htr in each of next 2 sts, 2htr in next st] to end, slst in top of 2ch – 32 sts.

5th round: 2ch, 1htr in each of next 2 sts, 2htr in next st, [1htr in each of next 3 sts, 2htr in next st] to end, slst in top of 2ch – 40 sts.

6th to 8th rounds: 2ch, [1htr in next st] to end, slst in top of 2ch.

9th round: 2ch, 1htr in each of next 2 sts, htr2tog, [1htr in each of next 3 sts, htr2tog] to end, slst in top of 2ch – 32 sts.

10th to 12th rounds: 2ch, [1htr in next st] to end, slst in top of 2ch.

13th round: 2ch, 1htr in next st, htr2tog, [1htr in each of next 2 sts, htr2tog] to end, slst in top of 2ch – 24 sts.

14th to 16th rounds: 2ch, [1htr in next st] to end, slst in top of 2ch.

17th round: 2ch, htr2tog, [1htr in next st, htr2tog] to end, slst in top of 2ch – 16 sts. Stuff head.

18th round: 1ch (does not count as a st), miss first st, 1htr in next htr,

[htr2tog] to end – 8 sts.

Fasten off for lower head.

Gather fastened-off edge, pull up tightly and secure. With joins of rounds at back, position10th round of head to fastened- off edge of body and 16th round of head 4 rounds down from top of body front, then sew head in position. With Brown, embroider eyes and nostrils.

HORNS (MAKE 2)

1st round: With 3.00 hook, make slip ring as on first leg of lion, 1ch (does not count as st), work 8dc in ring, pull end of yarn tightly to close ring.

2nd round: [1dc in next st] 8 times.

3rd round: [Dc2tog] 4 times – 4 sts.

4th to 7th rounds: [1dc in next st] 4 times. Fasten off.

Sew horns to top of head.

EARS (MAKE 2)

With 3.00 hook, make 2ch.

1st round: 5htr in 2nd ch from hook, slst in first htr.

2nd round: 2ch, 1htr in base of 2ch, 2htr in next st, work 2htr, 2ch and 2htr all in next st, 2h tr in each of last 2 sts, slst in top of 2ch. Fasten off.

With pointed top uppermost, sew ears to top of head at sides of horns.

ARMS & TAIL

Work as given for lion.

Pig Plushie

This adorable pig is the perfect companion for anyone who loves cuddly toys

DIFFICULTY

✕ ✕ ✕ ✕

WHAT YOU NEED

- 4.00 crochet hook
- Small amount in Green for embroidery
- Washable toy stuffing

- Sublime Baby Cashmere Merino Silk DK (75% merino wool, 20% silk, 5% cashmere)
  Colour: 1 x 50g (116m) Piglet (01)

MEASUREMENTS

Approximately 24cm/9½in tall, excluding ears.

ABBREVIATIONS

Ch, chain; dc, double crochet; st, stitch; tr, treble; chsp, chain space; dc2tog, dc2 together [insert hook in next st, yarn over hook and draw through] twice, yarn over hook and draw loop through all 3 loops on hook; slst, slip stitch.

BODY

With 4.00 hook, make 2ch.

1st round: 6dc in 2nd ch from hook.

Mark end of last round and move this marker up at end of every round.

2nd round: [2dc in next st] 6 times – 12 sts.

3rd round: [2dc in next st, 1dc in next st] 6 times – 18 sts.

4th round: [2dc in next st, 1dc in each of next 2 sts] 6 times – 24 sts.

5th round: [2dc in next st, 1dc in each of next 3 sts] 6 times – 30 sts.

6th round: [2dc in next st, 1dc in each of next 4 sts] 6 times – 36 sts.

7th round: [2dc in next st, 1dc in each of next 5 sts] 6 times – 42 sts.

8th round: [2dc in next st, 1dc in each of next 6 sts] 6 times – 48 sts.

9th round: [2dc in next st, 1dc in each of next 7 sts] 6 times – 54 sts.

10th round: [1dc in next st] to end.

11th to 13th rounds: As 10th round.

14th round: [Dc2tog, 1dc in each of next 7 sts] 6 times – 48 sts.

15th to 17th rounds: As 10th round.

18th round: [Dc2tog, 1dc in each of next 6 sts] 6 times – 42 sts.

19th and 20th rounds: As 10th round.

21st round: [Dc2tog, 1dc in each of next 5 sts] 6 times – 36 sts.

22nd and 23rd rounds: As 10th round.

24th round: [Dc2tog, 1dc in each of next 4 sts] 6 times – 30 sts.

25th round: As 10th round.

26th round: [Dc2tog, 1dc in each of next 3 sts] 6 times – 24 sts.

27th round: As 10th round.

28th round: [Dc2tog, 1dc in each of next 2 sts] 6 times – 18 sts.

Stuff body firmly, adding more stuffing as you working last 2 rounds.

29th round: [Dc2tog, 1dc in next st] 6 times – 12 sts.

30th round: [Dc2tog] 6 times – 6 sts.

Fasten off for top edge.

Gather fastened-off edge, pull up tightly and secure.

HEAD

With 4.00 hook, make 2ch.

1st round: 6dc in 2nd ch from hook.

Mark end of last round and move this marker up at end of every round.

2nd round: [2dc in next st] 6 times – 12 sts.

3rd round: [2dc in next st, 1dc in next st] 6 times – 18 sts.

4th round: Working in back loop of every st, [1dc in next st] to end.

5th to 7th rounds: [1dc in next st] to end.

8th round: [2dc in next st, 1dc in each of next 2 sts] 6 times – 24 sts.

9th round: [1dc in next st] to end.

10th round: [2dc in next st, 1dc in each of next 3 sts] 6 times – 30 sts.

11th round: As 9th round.

12th round: [2dc in next st, 1dc in each of next 4 sts] 6 times – 36 sts.

13th round: As 9th round.

14th round: [2dc in next st, 1dc in each of next 5 sts] 6 times – 42 sts.

15th round: [2dc in next st, 1dc in each of next 6 sts] 6 times – 48 sts.

16th to 19th rounds: As 9th round.

20th round: [Dc2tog, 1dc in each of next 6 sts] 6 times – 42 sts.

21st round: [Dc2tog, 1dc in each of next 5 sts] 6 times – 36 sts.

22nd round: [Dc2tog, 1dc in each of next 4 sts] 6 times – 30 sts.

23rd round: [Dc2tog, 1dc in each of next 3 sts] 6 times – 24 sts.

24th round: [Dc2tog, 1dc in each of next 2 sts] 6 times – 18 sts.

Stuff head firmly.

25th round: [Dc2tog, 1dc in next st] 6 times – 12 sts.

26th round: [Dc2tog] 6 times – 6 sts.

Fasten off for back of head.

Gather fastened-off edge, pull up tightly and secure.

Sew head to top of body.

With Green, embroider eyes.

LEGS (MAKE 2)

With 4.00 hook, make 2ch.

1st round: 6dc in 2nd ch from hook.

Mark end of last round and move this marker up at end of every round.

2nd round: [2dc in next st] 6 times – 12 sts.

3rd to 14th rounds: [1dc in next st] to end. Fasten off.

Stuff legs, flatten tops and sew to base of body.

ARMS (MAKE 2)

With 4.00 hook, make 2ch.

1st round: 6dc in 2nd ch from hook.

Mark end of last round and move this marker up at end of every round.

2nd round: [2dc in next st] 6 times – 12 sts.

3rd to 11th rounds: [1dc in next st] to end. Fasten off.

Stuff arms, flatten tops and sew to sides of body. Stitch hands together at centre front

TAIL

With 4.00 hook, make 11ch.

1st row: 1dc in 2nd ch from hook, 1dc in each of next 9ch. Fasten off.

Allowing tail to curl as much as possible, sew end to back of body

EARS (MAKE 2)

With 4.00 hook, make 3ch.

1st row: 2tr in 3rd ch from hook, turn.

2nd row: 1ch (does not count as a st), 2dc in first st, 1dc in next st, 2dc in last dc, turn – 5 sts.

3rd row: 3ch, 1tr in base of 3ch, [miss next st, 2tr in next st] twice, turn – 6 sts.

4th row: 1ch, 2dc in first st, 1dc in each of 5 sts, turn – 7 sts.

5th row: 3ch, 1tr in base of 3ch, [miss next st, 2tr in next st] 3 times – 8 sts. Fasten off. Sew fastened off edges to sides of head.

FLOWER

With 4.00 hook, make 6ch, slst in first ch to form a ring.

1st round: 3ch (counts as 1dc and 2ch), into ring work [1dc, 2ch] 5 times, slst in first of 3ch.

2nd round: Slst in first chsp, work 1dc, 3tr and 1dc in first chsp, [work 1dc, 3tr and 1dc in next chsp] 5 times, slst in first dc, then make 10ch for stem. Fasten off.

Attach top of flower stem to hands.

PATTERN NOTES

• Yarn amounts are based on average requirements and are therefore approximate. Instructions in square brackets are worked as stated after 2nd bracket.

Octopus Plushie

This tactile octopus toy is fun for little hands to play with

DIFFICULTY

✕ ✕ ✕ ✕

WHAT YOU NEED

• 3.5mm crochet hook
• Stitch marker
• Washable toy stuffings
• Stylecraft Special DK

Colour 1: 1 x 100g (295m) Blush (1833)
Colour 2: Oddment Black (1002)

MEASUREMENTS

Approx 20cm/8in long (with tentacles laid out flat).

TENSION

20 stitches and 21 rounds, to 10 x 10cm, over

double crochet, using 3.5mm hook.

ABBREVIATIONS

Ch, chain; st(s), stitch(es);
dc, double crochet; yrh, yarn round hook; dc2tog,
double crochet 2 sts together (to decrease 1 st)
thus: [insert hook into st or space as indicated, yrh,
and pull a loop through] twice, yrh and pull through
all 3 loops on hook.

PATTERN

BODY

Starting at top.

With 3.5mm hook and Pink, make 2ch.

1st round: 6dc in 2nd ch from hook –6 sts.

Place st marker in last st, and move this up at end of each round.

2nd round: [2dc in next st] to end – 12 sts.

3rd round: [2dc in next st, 1dc in next st] to end – 18 sts.

4th round: [2dc in next st, 1dc in each of next 2 sts] to end – 24 sts.

5th round: [2dc in next st, 1dc in each of next 3 sts] to end – 30 sts.

6th round: [2dc in next st, 1dc in each of next 4 sts] to end – 36 sts.

7th round: [2dc in next st, 1dc in each of next 5 sts] to end – 42 sts.

8th to 19th rounds: [1dc in next st] to end.

20th round: [Dc2tog, 1dc in each of next 5 sts] to end – 36 sts.

21st round: [1dc in next st] to end.

22nd round: [Dc2tog, 1dc in each of next 4 sts] to end – 30 sts.

23rd round: [Dc2tog, 1dc in each of next 3 sts] to end – 24 sts.

24th round: [Dc2tog, 1dc in each of next 2 sts] to end – 18 sts.

25th round: [Dc2tog, 1dc in next st] to end – 12 sts.

Stuff body.

26th round: [Dc2tog] to end – 6 sts.

Fasten off. Add more stuffing if required then close gap in body.

TENTACLES

With 3.5mm hook and Pink, make 70ch.

1st row: 1dc in 2nd ch from hook, [1dc in next ch] to end – 69 sts.

2nd row: 1ch (does not count as a st), [dc2tog, 1dc in next st] to end – 46 sts.

3rd row: 1ch (does not count as a st), [dc2tog, 1dc in next st] to last st, 1dc in last st – 31 sts.

Fasten off.

TO MAKE UP

Pin one end of each tentacle to underside of body so they are evenly spaced. Sew in place. With Black, embroider a few vertical stitches for the eyes and sew a small 'V' for the mouth to make a cute expression.

PATTERN NOTES

• Body is made in rounds that are worked in a continuous spiral. Place stitch marker at the end of each round and move this up as you work. When working in rounds, the right side is on the outside. Yarn amounts are based on average requirements and are therefore approximate. Instructions in square brackets are worked as stated after 2nd bracket.

DESImiddleGNED BY

MEVLINN
GUSICK

Mevlinn is a college graduate with
a BFA in Fine Arts Painting. Her
interest in knitting and crochet
began when her aunt suggested
she try knitting. It peaked her
curiosity and here she is today,
crocheting amigurumi whenever
she gets the chance and giving
them to those she loves.
www.mevvsan.com

PATTERN NOTES

• The body has a side specific
decrease. This decrease is creating the
'rump' of the unicorn. Keep this in mind
when you sew the head
on later.

Magical Unicorn

Learn how to easily bring this much-loved fantasy creature into the real world – horn and all!

DIFFICULTY
✂ ✂ ✂ ✂

WHAT YOU NEED
• 2.75mm crochet hook
• Stitch marker
• Washable toy stuffings
• 9mm black safety eyes
• Aran weight yarn

Colour 1: 1 x 100g (295m) White
Colour 2: Oddment Dark Pink
Colour 3: Oddment Grey
Colour 4: Oddment Yellow
Colour 5: Oddment Light Pink

MEASUREMENTS
28 cm tall.

ABBREVIATIONS
St(s), stitch(es); dc, double crochet; yrh, yarn round hook; dc2tog, double crochet 2 sts together (to decrease 1 st) thus: [insert hook into st or space as indicated, yrh, and pull a loop through] twice, yrh and pull through all 3 loops on hook.

PATTERN
BODY
Using col 1, make a magic ring.

1st round: 7 dc in magic ring. (7 sts)

Place st marker in last st, and move this up at end of each round.

2nd round: 2 dc in each st around. (14 sts)

3rd round: (2 dc in next st, 1 dc in next st) 7 times. (21 sts)

4th round: (2 dc in next st, 1 dc in next 2 sts) 7 times. (28 sts).

5th round: (2 dc in next st, 1 dc in next 3 sts) 7 times. (35 sts)

6th round: (2 dc in next st, 1 dc in next 4 sts) 7 times. (42 sts)

7th round: 1 dc in each st around. (42 sts)

8th round: (2 dc in next st, dc in next 5 sts) 7 times. (49 sts)

9th round: 1 dc in each st around. (49 sts)

10th to 12th round: dc2tog, 1 dc in each remaining st. (46 sts after rnd 12)

13th to 14th round: dc2tog, 1 dc in each st to the last 3 sts, dc2tog, 1 dc in last st. (42 sts after rnd 14)

Stuff with fibrefill and continue stuffing as you go.

15th to 22nd round: dc2tog, 1 dc in each st to the last 3 sts, dc2tog, 1 dc in last st. (26 sts after rnd 22)

23rd to 28th round: dc2tog, 1 dc in each remaining st. (20 sts after rnd 28)

Fasten off leaving a tail for sewing. When the head is complete you will use this yarn end to sew the body and head together.

HEAD
Using col 1, make a magic ring.

1st round: 6 dc in magic ring. (6 sts)

2nd round: 2 dc in each st around. (12 sts)

3rd round: (2 dc in next st, 1 dc in next st) 6 times. (18 sts)

4th round: (2 dc in next st, 1 dc in next 2 sts) 6 times. (24 sts)

5th round: (2 dc in next st, 1 dc in next 3 sts) 6 times. (30 sts)

6th round: (2 dc in next st, 1 dc in next 4 sts) 6 times. (36 sts)

7th to 15th round: 1 dc in each st around. (8 rnds of 36 sts)

Change to col 2.

16th round: (2 dc in next st, 1 dc in next 5 sts) 6 times. (42 sts)

Place eyes between rnds 12 and 13 with 10 sts between the eyes.

17th to 21st round: 1 dc in each st around. (5 rnds of 42 sts)

Stuff with fibrefill and continue stuffing as you go.

22nd round: (dc2tog, 1 dc in next 5 sts) 6 times. (36 sts)

23rd round: (dc2tog, 1 dc in next 4 sts) 6 times. (30 sts)

24th round: (dc2tog, 1 dc in next 3 sts) 6 times. (24 sts)

25th round: (dc2tog, 1 dc in next 2 sts) 6 times. (18 sts)

26th round: (dc2tog, 1 dc in next st) 6 times. (12 sts)

27th round: (dc2tog) 6 times. (6 sts)

Fasten off, leaving a long tail for sewing. Using your yarn needle, weave the yarn tail through the front ring of each remaining st and pull it tight to close. Sew head onto body. The back of the neck should sew onto rnd 6 of the head.

LEGS (MAKE 2)

Using col 3, make a magic ring.

1st round: 4 dc in magic ring. (4 sts)

2nd round: 2 dc in each st around. (8 sts)

3rd round: (2 dc in next st, 1 dc in next st) 4 times. (12 sts)

4th round: 1 dc in each st around. (12 sts)

Change to col 1

5th to 17th round: 1 dc in each st around. (13 rounds of 12 sts)

Fasten off, leaving a tail for sewing. Lightly stuff the legs with more stuffing near the hooves.

ASSEMBLE THE LEGS

Start by sewing the back legs first. Place the horse on a flat surface in the seated position that you will want it to be, and pin the legs to the sides of the body.

Attach the back legs at rnds 6-8 of the body with 12 sts between the initial attachment points of each leg. Sew each leg about 8 sts down the leg against the body to stop them from bowing out.

(See inset on previous page.)

When the hind legs are attached, the unicorn should be able to sit well on its own, and this helps when sewing the front legs. Attach the front legs at rnd 19 of the body with 4 sts between each leg. Sew each leg about 8 sts down the leg against the body to stop the front legs from bowing out.

EARS (MAKE 2)

Using col 1, ch 5.

1st row: 1 dc in 2nd ch from hook, 1 dc in next 2 ch, 4 dc in last ch, rotate and work along the opposite side of the foundation ch, 1 dc in next 3 ch, turn. (10 sts)

2nd row: ch 1 (not counted as a st), 1 dc in next 3 sts, 2 dc in next 4 sts, 1 dc in next 3 sts, turn. (14 sts)

3rd row: ch 1 (not counted as a st), 1 dc in each st around. (14 sts

Fasten off, leaving a tail for sewing. Pinch the base of the ear together

and sew the ears 6 rnds behind the eyes with 9 sts between each ear.

HORN

Using col 4, make a magic ring

1st round: 4 dc in magic ring. (4 sts)

2nd to 6th round (blo): 2 dc in next st, 1 dc in each remaining st. (9 sts after rnd 6)

Fasten off, leaving a long tail for sewing. Sew the horn unstuffed onto the top of the head between the ears and the eyes.

TAIL

Cut 5 strands each of col 2 and col 5 that are 30 cm in length. Take one strand of each col and fold them in half. With the folded end between your fingers, insert your hook in the rump of your unicorn where you want the tail to be (about rnd 8 of the body), and place the folded ends of the yarn onto the hook and pull them back through the body. Take the loose ends of the yarn, wrap them around the hook and pull them through the ring. Pull to tighten. Repeat this 4 more times in sts adjacent to the first st to create a thick tail.

Separate the strands into 3 sections and braid or plait them. Take a piece of col 4 and wrap it around the end of the braid, then tie it tightly with a bow.

MANE

Cut a few dozen strands each of cols 2 and 5 that are 25 cm in length. Find the centre of the unicorn's head and, using one strand at a time, attach the mane using the same method as given for the tail. To keep the mane straight, follow the sts down the back in a straight line until about 15 strands have been attached, alternating between col 2 and col 5. Repeat to add another line on each side of the centre mane to create 3 lines in total. Trim and braid or plait the mane.

You could make a multicoloured rainbow mane and tail

Crochet Letter 'B'

A brilliant addition to alphabet-based decor

PATTERN NOTES

• Yarn amounts are based on average requirements and are therefore approximate. Instructions in square brackets are worked as stated after 2nd bracket.

Gifts & Amigurumi

103

DIFFICULTY

✂ ✂ ✂ ✂

WHAT YOU NEED

- 4.00 crochet hook
- Stuffing
- Erika Knight Gossypium Cotton (100% cotton)

Colour 1: 1 x 50g (100m) Yellow (503)
Colour 2: 1 x 50g (100m) Blue (504)
Colour 3: 1 x 50g (100m) White (500)

MEASUREMENTS

Approximately 23cm/9in high and 17cm/6¾in wide.

ABBREVIATIONS

Ch, chain; st, stitch; dc, double crochet; dc2tog, [insert hook into next st, yarn round hook, pull yarn through] twice, yarn round hook and pull through all 3 loops on hook; slst, slip stitch

---

FRONT

Bottom: With 4.00 hook and Yellow, make 24ch.

1st row (right side): 1dc in 2nd ch from hook, [1dc in next ch] to end, turn – 23 sts.

2nd row: 1ch (does not count as a st throughout), [1dc in next st] to last st, 2dc in last st, turn.

3rd row: 1ch, 2dc in first st, [1dc in next st] to end, turn.

4th and 5th rows: As 2nd and 3rd rows – 27 sts.

6th to 9th rows: 1ch, [1dc in next st] to end, turn.

10th (dividing) row: 1ch, 1dc in each of first 9 sts, turn and work on these sts only for bottom left side.

Bottom left side: 11th to 15th rows: 1ch, [1dc in next st] to end, turn.

16th row: 1ch, [1dc in next st] to end, make 9ch for horizontal bar – 18 sts. Fasten off.

Bottom right side: 10th row: With wrong side facing, return to end of dividing row, miss next 9 sts, join yarn in next st, 1ch, 1dc in same place as join, [1dc in next st] to end – 9 sts.

11th to 16th rows: 1ch, [1dc in next st] to end, turn.

17th (joining) row: 1ch, 1dc in each of 9 sts of right side, 1dc in each of 9ch of centre horizontal bar, 1dc in each of 9 sts of left side, turn – 27 sts.

18th row: 1ch, [1dc in next st] to last 2 sts, dc2tog, turn.

19th row: 1ch, dc2tog, [1dc in next st] to end, turn.

20th and 21st rows: As 18th and 19th rows – 23 sts.

22nd row: 1ch, [1dc in next st] to last st, 2dc in last st, turn.

23rd row: 1ch, 2dc in first st, [1dc in next st] to end, turn.

24th and 25th rows: As 22nd and 23rd rows – 27 sts.

26th (dividing) row: 1ch, 1dc in each of first 9 sts, turn and work on these sts only for top left side.

Top left side: 27th to 31st rows: 1ch, [1dc in next st] to end, turn.

32nd row: 1ch, [1dc in next st] to end, make 9ch for horizontal bar – 18 sts. Fasten off.

Top right side: 26th row: With wrong side facing, return to end of last dividing row, miss next 9 sts, join yarn in next st, 1ch, 1dc in same place as join, [1dc in next st] to end – 9 sts.

27th to 32nd rows: 1ch, [1dc in next st] to end, turn.

Top: 33rd (joining) row: 1ch, 1dc in each of 9 sts of right side, 1dc in each of 9ch of centre horizontal bar, 1dc in each of 9 sts of left side, turn – 27 sts.

34th to 37th rows: 1ch, [1dc in next st] to end, turn.

38th row: 1ch, [1dc in next st] to last 2 sts, dc2tog, turn.

39th row: 1ch, dc2tog, [1dc in next st] to end, turn.

40th and 41st rows: As 38th and 39th rows – 23 sts. Fasten off.

Inner edgings: With right side facing and using 4.00 hook, join Yellow to right corner of central horizontal bar and work 1ch, 27dc evenly around one opening, slst in first dc.

Fasten off, leaving a 150cm end.

Work around other opening in same way.

Outer edging: With right side facing and using 4.00 hook, join Yellow to bottom left side corner, 1ch, 22dc along bottom edge, 41dc along right side row-ends, 21dc along top edge, 3dc in corner, 35dc along left side row-ends, 3dc in corner, slst in first dc – 125dc. Fasten off.

BACK

Using Blue, work as front.

INNER GUSSETS (MAKE 2)

With 4.00 hook and White, make 28ch.

1st row (right side): 1dc in 2nd ch from hook, [1dc in next ch] to end, turn – 27 sts.

2nd to 4th rows: 1ch, [1dc in next st] to end, turn. Fasten off.

OUTER GUSSET

With 4.00 hook and White, make 126ch.

1st row (right side): 1dc in 2nd ch from hook, [1dc in next ch] to end, turn – 125 sts.

2nd to 4th rows: 1ch, [1dc in next dc] to end, turn. Fasten off.

TO MAKE UP

Join row-end edges together on each gusset. Place wrong sides of front and one inner gusset together, with gusset seam in one corner.

With right side of front facing, using 4.00 hook and attached yarn, work slst through corresponding stitches of both layers together. Fasten off. Attach other inner gusset in same way.

Join outer gusset to front in same way. Join gussets to back as on front, stuffing the letter section by section as you join outer gusset.

You could create an entire abc

Caterpillar Plushie

This lovely long caterpillar is the perfect addition to any child's bedroom

DIFFICULTY

✕ ✕ ✕ ✕

WHAT YOU NEED

- 3.50 crochet hook
- Washable toy stuffing
- Length of Black DK yarn for embroidery
- Wendy Love It DK (100% acrylic)

Colour 1: 1 x 100g (220m) Yellow (5006)
Colour 2: 1 x 100g (220m) Red (5011)
Colour 3: 1 x 100g (220m) Cream (5002)
Colour 4: 1 x 100g (220m) Fuchsia (5010)
Colour 5: 1 x 100g (220m) Orange (5008)
Colour 6: 1 x 100g (220m) Purple (5009)

MEASUREMENTS

Approximately 55cm/21½in long.

ABBREVIATIONS

Ch, chain; st, stitch; htr, half treble; slst, slip stitch; htr2tog, work 2htr together thus: [yarn round hook, insert hook in next st, yarn round hook and pull through] twice, yarn round hook and pull through all 5 loops on hook.

HEAD & BODY

Head: 1st round: With 3.50 hook and Yellow, make slip ring as follows: wind yarn round index finger of left hand to form ring, insert hook into ring, yarn over hook and pull through, 1ch (does not count as st), work 8htr in ring, pull end of yarn tightly to close ring.

Mark end of last round and move marker up at end of every round.

2nd round: [2htr in next st] 8 times – 16 sts.

3rd round: [2htr in next st, 1htr in next st] 8 times – 24 sts.

4th round: [2htr in next st, 1htr in each of next 2 sts] 8 times – 32 sts.

5th round: [2htr in next st, 1htr in each of next 3 sts] 8 times – 40 sts.

6th round: [2htr in next st, 1htr in each of next 4 sts] 8 times – 48 sts.

7th round: [1htr in next st] to end.

8th to 12th rounds: As 7th round.

13th round: [1htr in each of next 4 sts, htr2tog] 8 times – 40 sts.

14th round: [1htr in each of next 3 sts, htr2tog] 8 times – 32 sts.

15th round: [1htr in each of next 2 sts, htr2tog] 8 times – 24 sts.

16th round: [1htr in next st, htr2tog] 8 times – 16 sts. Fasten off.

Stuff head firmly.

Body: First segment: Join Red and work 3rd to 16th rounds. Fasten off. Stuff segment firmly.

Second segment: Join Cream and work 3rd to 16th rounds. Fasten off. Stuff segment firmly.

Third segment: Join Fuchsia and work 3rd to 16th rounds. Fasten off. Stuff segment firmly.

Fourth segment: Join Orange and work 3rd to 16th rounds. Fasten off. Stuff segment firmly.

Fifth segment: Join Purple and work 3rd to 16th rounds. Stuff segment firmly.

17th round: [Htr2tog] 8 times – 8 sts.

Fasten off.

Gather last round, pull up tightly and secure.

FEET

1st round: With 3.50 hook and Yellow, make slip ring as on head, 1ch (does not count as st), work 8htr in ring, pull end of yarn tightly to close ring.

Mark end of last round and move marker up at end of every round.

2nd round: [2htr in next st] 8 times – 16 sts.

3rd and 4th rounds: [1htr in next st] to end.

Stuff foot firmly.

5th round: [Htr2tog] 8 times – 8 sts. Fasten off.

Make 1 more foot in Yellow. Sew fastened-off edge of feet to Red segment of body.

Make a pair of feet in Red and sew to Cream segment of body.

Make a pair of feet in Cream and sew to Fuchsia segment of body.

Make a pair of feet in Fuchsia and sew to Orange segment of body.

Make a pair of feet in Orange and sew to Purple segment of body.

ANTENNA (MAKE 2)

1st round: With 3.50 hook and Red, make slip ring as on head, 1ch (does not count as st), work 8htr in ring, pull end of yarn tightly to close ring.

Mark end of last round and move marker up at end of every round.

2nd round: [2htr in next st, 1htr in next st] 4 times – 12 sts.

3rd round: [1htr in next st] to end.

Stuff antenna firmly, adding stuffing as you work.

4th round: [Htr2tog] 6 times – 6 sts.

Join in Yellow.

5th to 8th rounds: [1htr in next st] to end.

Slst in first st. Fasten off.

Sew fastened-off edge to top of head.

NOSE

1st round: With 3.50 hook and Red, make slip ring as on head, 1ch (does not count as st), work 8htr in ring, pull end of yarn tightly to close ring.

2nd round: [1htr in next st] to end, slst in first st. Fasten off.

Stuff firmly. Sew fastened-off edge to front of face.

EYES (MAKE 2)

1st round: With 3.50 hook and Cream, make slip ring as on head, 1ch (does not count as st), work 8htr in ring, pull end of yarn tightly to close ring, slst in first st. Fasten off.

Sew to front of head. With Black, embroider pupil on each eye, then work long straight stitch on head below nose for mouth.

PATTERN NOTES

- Yarn amounts are based on average requirements and are therefore approximate. Instructions in square brackets are worked as stated after 2nd bracket.

With Much Love...

Blanket, bootees and toy – gifts galore for a newborn babe

DIFFICULTY

✕ ✕ ✕ ✕

WHAT YOU NEED

- 3.50 crochet hook
- Length of Black yarn for embroidery
- Washable toy stuffings
- Rico Design Baby Cotton Soft DK
  (50% cotton, 50% acrylic)
- Colour 1: 4 x 50g (125m) White (001)

Colour 2: 4 x 50g (125m) Lobster (029)

Colour 3: 4 x 50g (125m) Mint (031)

MEASUREMENTS

Blanket: Approximately 67 x 77cm/60½ x 30¼in.

Bootees: To fit ages 3-6 months.

Toy: 15cm/6in wide and 13cm/5in high.l

TENSION

22 stitches and 25 rows, to 10 x 10cm, over double

crochet, using 3.50 hook.

ABBREVIATIONS

Ch, chain; st, stitch; dc, double crochet; tr, treble; htr, half treble; slst, slip st; chsp, chain space; yrh, yarn round hook; dc2tog, work 2dc together thus: [insert hook in next st, yrh and pull through] twice, yrh and pull through all 3 loops on hook; tr2tog, work 2tr together thus: [yrh, insert hook in next st, yrh and pull through, yrh and pull through first 2 loops on hook] twice, yrh and pull through all 3 loops on hook.

BLANKET
MOTIF (MAKE 42)

With 3.50 hook and Mint, make 21ch.

1st row: 1dc in 2nd ch from hook (counts as 1 st), 1dc in each ch to end, turn – 20dc.

Twisting yarns together on wrong sides when changing colours and working last dc before colour change as follows: with yarn used, insert hook in next dc, yrh and pull through, with next colour, yrh and pull through 2 loops on hook, continue thus:

2nd row: With Mint, 1ch (does not count as a st throughout), 1dc in each of first 19dc, with White, 1dc in last dc, turn.

3rd row: With White, 1ch, 1dc in each of first 2dc, with Mint, 1dc in each of last 18dc, turn.

4th row: With Mint, 1ch, 1dc in each of first 17dc, with White, 1dc in each of last 3dc, turn.

5th row: With White, 1ch, 1dc in each of first 4dc, with Mint, 1dc in each of last 16dc, turn.

6th row: With Mint, 1ch, 1dc in each of first 15dc, with White, 1dc in each of last 5dc, turn.

7th row: With White, 1ch, 1dc in each of first 6dc, with Mint, 1dc in each of last 14dc, turn.

8th row: With Mint, 1ch, 1dc in each of first 13dc, with White, 1dc in each of last 7dc, turn.

9th row: With White, 1ch, 1dc in each of first 8dc, with Mint, 1dc in each of last 12dc, turn.

10th row: With Mint, 1ch, 1dc in each of first 11dc, with White, 1dc in each of last 9dc, turn.

11th row: With White, 1ch, 1dc in each of first 10dc, with Mint, 1dc in each of last 10dc, turn.

12th row: With Mint, 1ch, 1dc in each of first 9dc, with White, 1dc in each of last 11dc, turn.

13th row: With White, 1ch, 1dc in each of first 12dc, with Mint, 1dc in each of last 8dc, turn.

14th row: With Mint, 1ch, 1dc in each of first 7dc, with White, 1dc in each of last 13dc, turn.

15th row: With White, 1ch, 1dc in each of first 14dc, with Mint, 1dc in each of last 6dc, turn.

16th row: With Mint, 1ch, 1dc in each of first 5dc, with White, 1dc in each of last 15dc, turn.

17th row: With White, 1ch, 1dc in each of first 16dc, with Mint, 1dc in each of last 4dc, turn.

18th row: With Mint, 1ch, 1dc in each of first 3dc, with White, 1dc in each of last 17dc, turn.

19th row: With White, 1ch, 1dc in each of first 18dc, with Mint, 1dc in each of last 2dc, turn.

*If you like, choose colours
to match baby's nursery*

20th row: With Mint, 1ch, 1dc in first dc, with White 1dc in each of last 19dc, turn.

21st row: With White, 1ch, 1dc in each of 20dc. Fasten off.

Edging: With right side facing and using 3.50 hook, join Lobster to first ch on base chain of motif and work 1dc in each of 20ch, 1ch for corner, 20dc along row-end edge, 1ch for corner, 1dc in each of 20dc along fastened off edge, 1ch for corner, 20dc along other row-end edge, 1ch for corner, slst in first dc.

Next round: [1dc in each dc to corner chsp, work 1dc, 1ch and 1dc all in corner chsp] 4 times, slst in first dc. Fasten off.

TO MAKE UP

Arrange motifs in 6 rows of 7 motifs each. Working horizontally, place motifs with wrong sides together, using 3.50 hook and Lobster, joining motifs by working slst into back loops of each corresponding pair of stitches. Join motifs vertically in same way.

Border: With right side facing and using 3.50 hook, join Lobster with slst to any corner chsp, 3ch (counts as 1tr), * 1tr in each of next 21dc, [tr2tog over next dc and chsp, tr2tog over next chsp and dc, 1dc in each of next 20dc] to last motif before corner, tr2tog over next dc and chsp, tr2tog over next chsp and dc, 1dc in each of next 21dc, work 1tr, 1ch, 1tr, 1ch and 1tr all in corner chsp, repeat from * 3 times more, ending with work 1tr, 1ch, 1tr and 1ch all in same chsp as slst, slst in top of 3ch – 592 sts.

Next 3 rounds: 3ch, [1tr in each tr to first chsp at corner, 1tr in chsp, work 1tr, 1ch, 1tr, 1ch and 1tr all in next tr, 1tr in next chsp] 4 times, slst in top of 3ch. Fasten off and neaten ends.

BOOTEES
MOTIF (MAKE 2)

Sides and heel: With 3.50 hook and White, make 37ch.

1st row: 1dc in 2nd ch from hook, 1dc in each ch to end, turn – 36dc.

2nd to 5th rows: 1ch (does not count as a st throughout), 1dc in each dc to end, turn.

6th row: 3ch (counts as 1tr throughout), 1tr in each of next 6dc, 1htr in next dc, 1dc in each of next 20dc, 1htr in next dc, 1tr in each of last 7dc, turn.

7th row: 3ch, 1tr in each of next 7 sts, 1htr in next st, 1dc in each of next 18 sts, 1htr in next st, 1tr in each of last 8 sts, turn.

8th row: 1ch, 1htr in next st, [1ch, miss 1 st, 1htr in next st] to last st, slst in last st. Fasten off.

Instep: With 3.50 hook and Mint, make 23ch.

1st row: 1dc in 2nd ch from hook, 1dc in each ch to end, turn – 22dc.

2nd to 5th rows: 1ch, 1dc in each of next 5 sts, dc2tog, [1dc in next st] to last 7dc, dc2tog, 1dc in each of last 5 sts, turn – 14 sts.

6th row: 1ch, 1dc in each of next 5 sts, [dc2tog twice, 1dc in each of last 5dc, turn – 12 sts.

7th row: 1ch, 1dc in each of next 5 sts, dc2tog, 1dc in each of last 5 sts, turn – 11 sts.

8th row: 1ch, 1dc in each of next 3 sts, dc2tog, 1dc in next st, dc2tog, 1dc in each of last 3 sts, turn – 9 sts.

9th row: 1ch, [miss 1 st, insert hook in next st, yrh and pull through] 4 times, yrh and pull through all 5 loops on hook, slst in last st. Fasten off.

Sole: With 3.50 hook and White, make 13ch.

1st round: 2dc in 2nd ch from hook, 1dc in each of next 10ch, 3dc in last ch, now work along other side of chain thus: 1dc in each of next 11ch, slst in first dc – 26dc.

2nd round: 1ch, 1dc in same dc as slst, 2dc in next dc, 1dc in each of next 10dc, 2dc in next dc, 1dc in next dc, 2dc in next dc, 1dc in each of next 10dc, 2dc in last dc, slst in first dc – 30dc.

3rd round: 1ch, 1dc in same dc as slst, 2dc in next dc, 1dc in each of next 12dc, 2dc in next dc, 1dc in next dc, 2dc in next dc, 1dc in each of next 12dc, 2dc in last dc, slst in first dc – 34dc.

4th round: 1ch, 1dc in same dc as slst, 2dc in next dc, 1dc in each of next 14dc, 2dc in next dc, 1dc in next dc, 2dc in next dc, 1dc in each of next 14dc, 2dc in last dc, slst in first dc – 38dc.

Shape front: 5th round: 3ch, 2tr in next st, 1tr in next st, 2tr in next st, 1tr in each of next 4 sts, 1htr in next st, 1dc in each of next 5 sts, 1htr in each of next 2 sts, 2htr in next st, [1htr in next st, 2htr in next st] 3 times, 1htr in each of next 2 sts, 1dc in each of next 5 sts, 1htr in next st, 1tr in each of next 4 sts, 2tr in next st, 1tr in next st, 2tr in last st, slst in top of 3ch – 46 sts.

6th round: 3ch, 2htr in next st, [1htr in next st, 2htr in next st] twice, 1htr in each of next 4 sts, 1dc in each of next 7 sts, 1htr in each of next 3 sts, 2htr in next st, [1htr in next st, 2htr in next st] 3 times, 1htr in each of next 3 sts, 1dc in each of next 7 sts, 1htr in each of next 4 sts, [2htr in next st, 1htr in next st] twice, 2htr in last st, slst in top of 3ch – 56 sts. Fasten off.

TO MAKE UP

With right side facing, using 3.50 hook and Lobster, join row-ends at each side of instep to row-ends of sides and heel with slst, leaving last row on top free.

With right side facing, using 3.50 hook and Lobster join sole in place by working slst into back loops of each corresponding pair of stitches. With Lobster, make two 30cm-long twisted cords. Thread each along top edge, bringing ends at front.

TOY
BODY

With 3.50 hook and White, make 42ch, making sure that the chain is not twisted, slst in first ch to form ring.

1st round: 1dc in each ch to end, slst in first dc.

2nd round: 1ch (does not count as a st throughout entire instructions), [2dc in next dc, 1dc in each of next 6dc] 6 times, slst in first dc – 48 sts.

3rd round: 1ch, [2dc in next dc, 1dc in each of next 7dc] 6 times, slst in first dc – 54 sts.

4th round: 1ch, [2dc in next dc, 1dc in each of next 8dc] 6 times, slst in first dc – 60 sts.

5th round: 1ch, [2dc in next dc, 1dc in each of next 9dc] 6 times, slst in first dc – 66 sts.

6th round: 1ch, [2dc in next dc, 1dc in each of next 10dc] 6 times, slst in first dc – 72 sts.

7th round: 1ch, [2dc in next dc, 1dc in each of next 11dc] 6 times, slst in first dc – 78 sts.

8th to 10th rounds: 1ch, 1dc in each dc to end, slst in first dc.

11th round: 1ch, [dc2tog, 1dc in each of next 11 sts] 6 times, slst in first st – 72 sts.

12th round: 1ch, [dc2tog, 1dc in each of next 10 sts] 6 times, slst in first st – 66 sts.

13th round: 1ch, [dc2tog, 1dc in each of next 9 sts] 6 times, slst in first st – 60 sts.

14th round: 1ch, [dc2tog, 1dc in each of next 8 sts] 6 times, slst in first st – 54 sts.

15th round: 1ch, [dc2tog, 1dc in each of next 7 sts] 6 times, slst in first st – 48 sts.

16th round: 1ch, [dc2tog, 1dc in each of next 6 sts] 6 times, slst in first st – 42 sts.

Fasten off.

Join chain edge and fastened-off edge together, stuffing body as you work.

SNOUT

With 3.50 hook and Mint, make 5ch.

1st round: 2dc in 2nd ch from hook, 1dc in each of next 2ch, 3dc in last ch, now work along other side of chain thus: 1dc in each of next 3ch, slst in first dc – 10dc.

2nd round: 1ch, 1dc in same dc as slst, 2dc in next dc, 1dc in each of next 2dc, 2dc in next dc, 1dc in next dc, 2dc in next dc, 1dc in each of next 2dc, 2dc in last dc, slst in first dc – 14dc.

3rd round: 1ch, 1dc in same dc as slst, 2dc in next dc, 1dc in each of

next 4dc, 2dc in next dc, 1dc in next dc, 2dc in next dc, 1dc in each of next 4dc, 2dc in last dc, slst in first dc – 18dc.

4th and 5th rounds: 1ch, 1dc in each dc to end, slst in first dc.

Fasten off.

Stuff and sew snout to centre at top of body. With Lobster, embroider nose on snout. Work French knot in Black on body at each side of snout for eyes.

EARS (MAKE 2)

1st round: With 3.50 hook and Lobster, make a slip ring as follows: wind yarn round index finger of left hand to form a ring, insert hook into ring, yarn over hook and pull through, 1ch, 6dc in ring, slst in 1ch, pull end of yarn tightly to close ring – 6dc.

Mark end of round and move marker up at end of every round.

2nd round: [2dc in next dc] 6 times – 12dc.

3rd round: [2dc in next dc, 1dc in next dc] 6 times – 18dc. **

4th round: [2dc in next dc, 1dc in each of next 2dc] 6 times – 24dc.

Fold ear in half.

Next row: 1ch, work through corresponding pair of stitches thus: [2dc in next st, 1dc in each of next 3 sts] 3 times. Fasten off.

Sew ears to top of body as shown in the photo.

ARMS (MAKE 2)

With White, work as ears to **.

4th and 5th rounds: [1dc in next dc] to end.

6th and 7th rounds: [Dc2tog, 1dc in next st] to end – 8 sts.

Fasten off.

Stuff arms lightly and sew fastened-off edge to each side of body as shown in photo.

PATTERN NOTES

• The body of each animal is made using the same ball body pattern. When adding features, use the photos as a guide and ensure you sew in all ends as you go. Yarn amounts are based on average requirements and are therefore approximate. Instructions in square brackets are worked as stated after 2nd bracket.

Amigurumi

Small, round and bouncy – your little ones
will fall in love with our collection of animal pals

DIFFICULTY

✕ ✕ ✕ ✕

WHAT YOU NEED

- 3mm crochet hook
- Washable toy stuffings
- DMC Natura Just Cotton (100% cotton)
  - Colour 1: 1 x 50g (155) Lime (89)
  - Colour 2: 1 x 50g (155) Pink (93)
  - Colour 3: 1 x 50g (155) Orange (104)
  - Colour 4: 1 x 50g (155) Lilac (102)

Colour 5: 1 x 50g (155) White (01)
Colour 6: 1 x 50g (155) Green (99)
Colour 7: 1 x 50g (155) Black (11)

MEASUREMENTS

Approximately 10cm/4in tall, excluding ears.

TENSION

Tension is not critical for this project. Use a smaller
hook than recommended for your yarn so that the
toy filling is not visible through the stitches.

ABBREVIATIONS

Ch, chain; st(s), stitch(es); dc, double crochet; slst,
slip stitch; dc2tog, double crochet 2 sts together (to
decrease 1 st) thus: [insert hook into next st, yarn
round hook and pull a loop through] twice, yarn
round hook and pull through all 3 loops on hook.

BALL BODY

1st round: With 3mm hook and specified colour, make a slip ring as follows,
wind yarn round index finger of left hand to form a ring, insert hook into ring,
yarn round hook and pull through, 1ch (does not count as a st throughout entire
pattern), work 8dc in ring, slst in 1ch, pull end of yarn tightly to close ring – 8 sts.

2nd round: 1ch, [2dc in next st] 8 times, slst in 1ch – 16 sts.

3rd round: 1ch, [2dc in next st, 1dc in next st] 8 times, slst in 1ch – 24 sts.

4th round: 1ch, [2dc in next st, 1dc in each of next 2 sts] 8 times, slst in 1ch
– 32 sts.

5th round: 1ch, [2dc in next st, 1dc in each of next 3 sts] 8 times, slst in 1ch
– 40 sts.

6th to 8th rounds: 1ch, [1dc in next st] 40 times, slst in 1ch.

9th round: 1ch, [2dc in next st, 1dc in each of next 4 sts] 8 times, slst in 1ch
– 48 sts.

10th round: 1ch, [2dc in next st, 1dc in each of next 5 sts] 8 times, slst in 1ch
– 56 sts.

11th to 14th rounds: 1ch, [1dc in next st] 56
times, slst in 1ch.

15th round: 1ch, [dc2tog, 1dc in each of next 5
sts] 8 times, slst in 1ch – 48 sts.

16th round: 1ch, [dc2tog, 1dc in each of next
4 sts] 8 times, slst in 1ch – 40 sts.

17th to 20th rounds: 1ch, [1dc in next st]
40 times, slst in 1ch.

Stuff firmly and continue to stuff as you work the last few rounds.

21st round: 1ch, [dc2tog, 1dc in each of next 3 sts] 8 times, slst in 1ch – 32 sts.

22nd round: 1ch, [dc2tog, 1dc in each of next 2 sts] 8 times, slst in 1ch – 24 sts.

23rd round: 1ch, [dc2tog, 1dc in next st] 8 times, slst in 1ch – 16 sts.

24th round: 1ch, [dc2tog] 8 times, slst in 1ch – 8 sts.

Fasten off leaving a long end. Weave end along top edge of last round, pull up
tightly and fasten off securely for base.

DUCK
BODY
With Lime, work as given for ball body.

EYES (MAKE 2)
1st round: With 3mm hook and Black, work as given for 1st round of ball body – 8 sts. Fasten off leaving a long end. Sew eyes in place.

BEAK (MAKE 2)
1st round: With 3mm hook and Orange, work as given for 1st round of ball body – 8 sts.

2nd to 4th rounds: 1ch, [1dc in next st] 8 times, slst in 1ch.

Fasten off leaving a long end. Flatten pieces. Join straight edges of the two pieces together to form beak. Sew beak in place.

FEET (MAKE 2)
With 3mm hook and Orange, make 8ch.

1st round: 1dc in 2nd ch from hook, 1dc in each of next 5ch, 3dc in next ch, do not turn, instead work along base edge of ch, 1dc in each of next 5ch, 2dc in next ch, slst in 1ch at beginning – 16 sts.

2nd round: 1ch, [1dc in next st] 16 times, slst in 1ch.

3rd round: 1ch, [dc2tog, 1dc in each of next 6 sts] twice, slst in 1ch – 14 sts.

4th round: 1ch, [dc2tog, 1dc in each of next 5 sts] twice, slst in 1ch – 12 sts.

5th round: 1ch, [dc2tog, 1dc in each of next 4 sts] twice, slst in 1ch – 10 sts.

6th round: 1ch, [dc2tog, 1dc in each of next 3 sts] twice, slst in 1ch – 8 sts.

7th round: 1ch, [dc2tog, 1dc in each of next 2 sts] twice, slst in 1ch – 6 sts.

Fasten off leaving a long end. Flatten feet and catch stitches of last round together. Catch inner edges on last round of feet together and sew feet in place.

CAT
BODY
With Orange, work as given for ball body.

EYES
With Green, work as given for duck's eyes. With Pink, embroider nose in straight stitches. With Black, embroider eyes and mouth as shown in photo.

EARS
With Orange, work as given for pig's ears.

FEET
With Orange, work as given for pig's feet.

TAIL
Starting at tip.

1st round: With 3mm hook and Orange, work as given for 1st round of ball body – 8 sts.

2nd round: 1ch, [2dc in next st] 8 times, slst in 1ch – 16 sts.

3rd to 6th rounds: 1ch, [1dc in next st] 16 times, slst in 1ch.

7th round: 1ch, [dc2tog, 1dc in next st] 5 times, 1dc in last st, slst in 1ch – 11 sts. Stuff firmly and continue to stuff as you go.

8th to 19th rounds: 1ch, [1dc in next st] 11 times, slst in 1ch.

Fasten off leaving a long end. Flatten last round and catch stitches together. Sew tail in place.

RABBIT
BODY
With Lilac, work as given for ball body.

EYES
Work as given for duck's eyes. With Black, embroider mouth with a 'V' stitch.

EARS (MAKE 2)
1st round: With 3mm hook and Lilac, work as given for 1st round of ball body – 8 sts.

2nd round: 1ch, [2dc in next st] 8 times, slst in 1ch – 16 sts.

3rd to 14th rounds: 1ch, [1dc in next st] 16 times, slst in 1ch.

Fasten off leaving a long end. Flatten last round and catch stitches together. Pinch ear together to form a tiny pleat and sew in place.

FRONT FEET ONLY (MAKE 2)
With Lilac, work as given for pig's feet.

TAIL
1st round: With 3mm hook and White, work as given for 1st round of ball body – 8 sts.

2nd round: 1ch, [2dc in next st] 8 times, slst in 1ch – 16 sts.

3rd and 4th rounds: 1ch, [1dc in next st] 16 times, slst in 1ch.

5th round: 1ch, [dc2tog] 8 times, slst in 1ch – 8 sts.

6th round: 1ch, [dc2tog] 4 times, slst in 1ch – 4 sts.

Fasten off leaving a long end. Stuff tail. Thread end along top of last round, pull up tightly and fasten off securely. Sew tail in place.

DOG
BODY
With White, work as given for ball body.

EYES
Work as given for duck's eyes. With Black, embroider nose in straight stitches.

TONGUE
1st round: With 3mm hook and Pink, work as given for 1st round of ball body – 8 sts. Fasten off leaving a long end. Sew tongue in place.

EARS
With Black, work as given for rabbit's ears.

FEET
With White, work as given for pig's feet.

TAIL

Starting at tip.

1st round: With 3mm hook and White, work as given for 1st round of ball body – 8 sts.

2nd to 11th rounds: 1ch, [1dc in next st] 8 times, slst in 1ch.

Fasten off leaving a long end. Stuff tail. Flatten last round and catch stitches together. Sew tail in plac

PIG
BODY

With Pink, work as given for ball body.

EYES

Work as given for duck's eyes.

SNOUT

1st round: With 3mm hook and Pink, work as given for 1st round of ball body – 8 sts.

2nd round: 1ch, [2dc in next st] 8 times, slst in 1ch – 16 sts.

3rd and 4th rounds: Work in back loop only, 1ch, [1dc in next st] 16 times, slst in 1ch.

Fasten off leaving a long end. Stuff and sew snout in place.

With Black, embroider a 'V' for mouth and two tiny straight stitches on snout for nostrils.

EARS (MAKE 2)

1st round: With 3mm hook and Pink, work as given for 1st round of ball body – 8 sts.

2nd and 3rd rounds: 1ch, [1dc in next st] 8 times, slst in 1ch.

4th round: 1ch, [1dc in each of next 2 sts, 2dc in next st] twice, 1dc in each of next 2 sts, slst in 1ch – 10 sts.

5th round: 1ch, [1dc in next st] 10 times, slst in 1ch.

6th round: 1ch, [1dc in each of next 3 sts, 2dc in next st] twice, 1dc in each of next 2 sts, slst in 1ch – 12 sts.

Fasten off leaving a long end. Flatten ears and sew in place.

FEET (MAKE 4)

1st round: With 3mm hook and Pink, work as given for 1st round of ball body – 8 sts.

2nd round: 1ch, [2dc in next st] 8 times, slst in 1ch – 16 sts.

3rd and 4th rounds: 1ch, [1dc in next st] 16 times, slst in 1ch.

Fasten off leaving a long end. Stuff and sew feet in place.

TAIL

With 3mm hook and Pink, make 9ch.

1st row: 5dc in 2nd ch from hook, [miss next ch, 5dc in next ch] 3 times, slst in last ch – 20 sts.

Fasten off leaving a long end. Sew tail in place.

FROG
BODY

With Green, work as given for ball body.

EYES (MAKE 2)

1st round: With 3mm hook and Black, work as given for 1st round of ball body – 8 sts.

Break off Black. Join in Green.

2nd round: 1ch, [2dc in next st] 8 times, slst in 1ch – 16 sts.

3rd and 4th rounds: 1ch, [1dc in next st] 16 times, slst in 1ch.

5th round: 1ch, [dc2tog] 8 times, slst in 1ch – 8 sts.

6th round: 1ch, [dc2tog] 4 times, slst in 1ch – 4 sts.

Fasten off leaving a long end. Stuff eyes. Thread end along top of last round, pull up tightly and fasten off securely. Sew eyes in place.

Using Black, embroider a 'V' stitch for mouth.

FEET (MAKE 2)

1st toe: 1st round: With 3mm hook and Green, make a slip ring as follows, wind yarn round index finger of left hand to form a ring, insert hook into ring, yarn round hook and pull through, 1ch (does not count as a st throughout), work 5dc in ring, slst in 1ch, pull end of yarn tightly to close ring – 5 sts.

2nd and 3rd rounds: 1ch, [1dc in next st] 5 times, slst in 1ch.

Fasten off.

2nd and 3rd toes: Work as 1st toe, but do not fasten off on 3rd toe.

Place toes in a row so from left to right you'll have 1st, 2nd and 3rd toe, in that order. Work across toes thus,

Join toes: 4th round: 1ch, 1dc in each of next 2 sts on 3rd toe, 1dc in each of next 2 sts on 2nd toe and 1dc in each of next 4 sts on 1st toe, 1dc in each of next 2 sts on opposite side of 2nd toe, 1dc in each of next 2 sts on opposite side of 3rd toe (and therefore missing 1 st of 2nd toe and 1 st of 3rd toe), slst in 1ch – 12 sts.

5th and 6th rounds: 1ch, [1dc in next st] 12 times, slst in 1ch.

7th round: 1ch, [dc2tog, 1dc in next st] 4 times, slst in 1ch – 8 sts.

8th round: 1ch, [dc2tog] 4 times, slst in 1ch – 4 sts.

Fasten off leaving a long end. Thread end along top of last round, pull up tightly and fasten off securely. Sew feet in place.

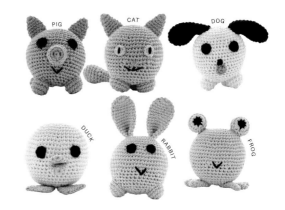

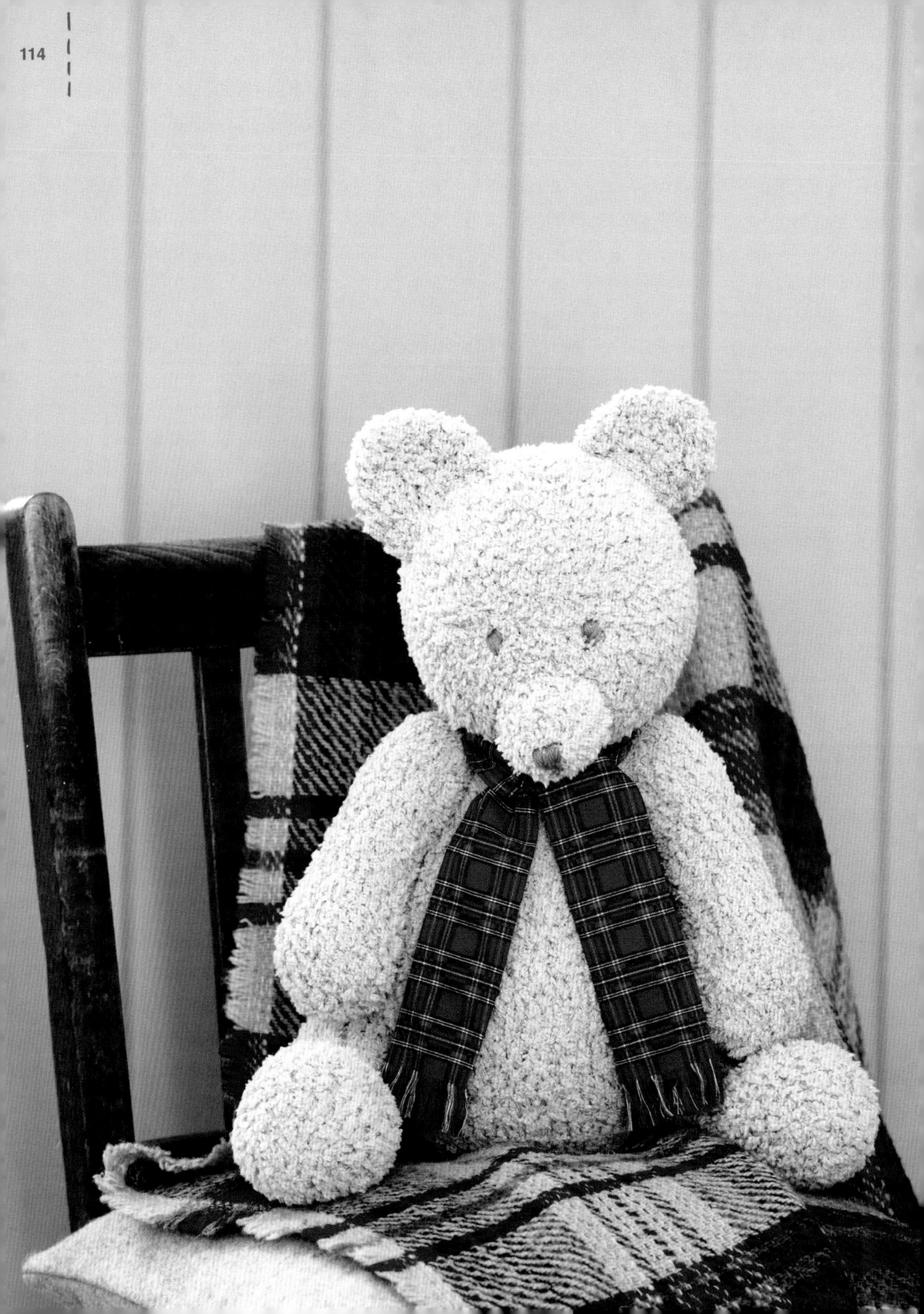

Huggy Bear

Meet our crocheted teddy bear – big, soft and oh-so cuddly!

DIFFICULTY

✕ ✕ ✕ ✕

WHAT YOU NEED

- 5.00 crochet hook
- Washable toy stuffing
- 67 x 11cm strip of tartan fabric
- Sewing needle and thread matching fabric
- Length of Light Brown for embroidery
- King Cole Cuddles DK (100% polyester)
  Colour: 3 x 50g (136m) Caramel (1184)
- King Cole Big Value Baby 4ply
  (100% acrylic)
  Colour: 1 x 100g (400m) Pebble (1681)

MEASUREMENTS

Approximately 53cm/21in tall.

ABBREVIATIONS

Ch, chain; st, stitch; htr, half treble; htr2tog, [yarn round hook, insert hook in next st, yarn round hook and pull through] twice, yarn round hook and pull through all 5 loops on hook; slst, slip stitch.

PATTERN

BODY

With 5.00 hook and one strand of Cuddles and one strand of 4ply together, make 2ch.

1st round: 5htr in 2nd ch, slst in first htr.

2nd round: 2ch, 1htr in base of 2ch, [2htr in next st] 4 times, slst in 2nd of 2ch – 10 sts.

3rd round: 2ch, 1htr in base of 2ch, [1htr in next st, 2htr in next st] 4 times, 1htr in last st, slst in 2nd of 2ch – 15 sts.

4th round: 2ch, 1htr in base of 2ch, [1htr in each of next 2 sts, 2htr in next st] 4 times, 1htr in each of last 2 sts, slst in 2nd of 2ch – 20 sts.

5th round: 2ch, 1htr in base of 2ch, [1htr in each of next 3 sts, 2htr in next st] 4 times, 1htr in each of last 3 sts, slst in 2nd of 2ch – 25 sts.

6th round: 2ch, 1htr in base of 2ch, [1htr in each of next 4 sts, 2htr in next st] 4 times, 1htr in each of last 4 sts, slst in 2nd of 2ch – 30 sts.

7th round: 2ch, 1htr in base of 2ch, [1htr in each of next 5 sts, 2htr in next st] 4 times, 1htr in each of last 5 sts, slst in 2nd of 2ch – 35 sts.

8th round: 2ch, 1htr in base of 2ch, [1htr in each of next 6 sts, 2htr in next st] 4 times, 1htr in each of last 6 sts, slst in 2nd of 2ch – 40 sts.

9th round: 2ch, 1htr in base of 2ch, [1htr in each of next 7 sts, 2htr in next st] 4 times, 1htr in each of last 7 sts, slst in 2nd of 2ch – 45 sts.

10th round: 2ch, [1htr in next st] to end, slst in 2nd of 2ch.

11th to 13th rounds: As 10th round.

14th round: 2ch, 1htr in each of next 6 sts, [htr2tog, 1htr in each of next 7 sts] 4 times, htr2tog, slst in 2nd of 2ch – 40 sts.

15th and 16th rounds: As 10th round.

17th round: 2ch, 1htr in each of next 5 sts, [htr2tog, 1htr in each of next 6 sts] 4 times, htr2tog, slst in 2nd of 2ch – 35 sts.

18th round: As 10th round.

19th round: 2ch, 1htr in each of next 4 sts, [htr2tog, 1htr in each of next 5 sts] 4 times, htr2tog, slst in 2nd of 2ch – 30 sts.

20th round: As 10th round.

21st round: 2ch, 1htr in each of next 3 sts, [htr2tog, 1htr in each of next 4 sts] 4 times, htr2tog, slst in 2nd of 2ch – 25 sts.

22nd round: As 10th round.

23rd round: 2ch, 1htr in each of next 2 sts, [htr2tog, 1htr in each of next 3 sts] 4 times, htr2tog, slst in 2nd of 2ch – 20 sts.

24th round: As 10th round.

25th round: 2ch, 1htr next st, [htr2tog, 1htr in each of next 2 sts] 4 times, htr2tog, slst in 2nd of 2ch – 15 sts. Fasten off.

Stuff body. Gather top edge, pull up tightly and secure.

HEAD

With 5.00 hook and one strand of Cuddles and one strand of 4ply together, make 2ch.

1st round: 6htr in 2nd ch, slst in first htr.

2nd round: 2ch, 1htr in base of 2ch, [2htr in next st] 5 times, slst in 2nd of 2ch – 12 sts.

3rd round: 2ch, 1htr in base of 2ch, [1htr in next st, 2htr in next st] 5 times, 1htr in last st, slst in 2nd of 2ch – 18 sts.

4th round: 2ch, 1htr in base of 2ch, [1htr in each of next 2 sts, 2htr in next st] 5 times, 1htr in each of last 2 sts, slst in 2nd of 2ch – 24 sts.

5th round: 2ch, 1htr in base of 2ch, [1htr in each of next 3 sts, 2htr in next st] 5 times, 1htr in each of last 3 sts, slst in 2nd of 2ch – 30 sts.

6th round: 2ch, 1htr in base of 2ch, [1htr in each of next 4 sts, 2htr in next st] 5 times, 1htr in each of last 4 sts, slst in 2nd of 2ch – 36 sts.

7th round: 2ch, 1htr in base of 2ch, [1htr in each of next 5 sts, 2htr in next st] 5 times, 1htr in each of last 5 sts, slst in 2nd of 2ch – 42 sts.

8th to 13th rounds: 2ch, [1htr in next st] to end, slst in 2nd of 2ch.

14th round: 2ch, 1htr in each of next 4 sts, [htr2tog, 1htr in each of next 5 sts] 5 times, htr2tog, slst in 2nd of 2ch – 36 sts.

15th round: 2ch, 1htr in each of next 3 sts, [htr2tog, 1htr in each of next 4 sts] 5 times, htr2tog, slst in 2nd of 2ch – 30 sts.

16th round: 2ch, 1htr in each of next 2 sts, [htr2tog, 1htr in each of next 3 sts] 5 times, htr2tog, slst in 2nd of 2ch – 24 sts.

17th round: 2ch, 1htr in next st, [htr2tog, 1htr in each of next 2 sts] 5 times, htr2tog, slst in 2nd of 2ch – 18 sts. Stuff head and continue to stuff as you go.

18th round: 2ch, [htr2tog, 1htr in next st] 5 times, htr2tog, slst in 2nd of 2ch – 12 sts. Fasten off.

Gather top edge, pull up tightly and secure. Sew head to top of body.

LEGS (MAKE 2)

With 5.00 hook and one strand of Cuddles and one strand of 4ply together, make 2ch.

1st round: 6htr in 2nd ch, slst in first htr.

2nd round: 2ch, 1htr in base of 2ch, [2htr in next st] 5 times, slst in 2nd of 2ch – 12 sts.

3rd round: 2ch, 1htr in base of 2ch, [1htr in next st, 2htr in next st] 5 times, 1htr in last st, slst in 2nd of 2ch – 18 sts.

4th round: 2ch, 1htr in base of 2ch, [1htr in each of next 2 sts, 2htr in next st] 5 times, 1htr in each of last 2 sts, slst in 2nd of 2ch – 24 sts.

5th round: 2ch, [1htr in next st] to end, slst in 2nd of 2ch.

6th to 8th rounds: As 5th round.

9th round: 2ch, 1htr in each of next 6 sts, [htr2tog] 5 times, 1htr in each of next 7 sts, slst in 2nd of 2ch – 19 sts.

10th to 18th rounds: As 5th round.

Stuff leg and continue to stuff as you go.

19th round: 2ch, [htr2tog] 9 times, slst in 2nd of 2ch – 10 sts.

Fasten off.

Gather top edge, pull up tightly and secure.

Sew tops of legs to sides of body at hip position.

ARMS (MAKE 2)

With 5.00 hook and one strand of Cuddles and one strand of 4ply together, make 2ch.

1st round: 6htr in 2nd ch, slst in first htr.

2nd round: 2ch, 1htr in base of 2ch, [2htr in next st] 5 times, slst in 2nd of 2ch – 12 sts.

3rd round: 2ch, 1htr in base of 2ch, [1htr in next st, 2htr in next st] 5 times, 1htr in last st, slst in 2nd of 2ch – 18 sts.

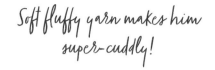

Soft fluffy yarn makes him super-cuddly!

4th round: 2ch, [1htr in next st] to end, slst in 2nd of 2ch.

5th round: As 4th round.

6th round: 2ch, 1htr in each of next 3 sts, [htr2tog, 1htr in each of next 4 sts] twice, htr2tog, slst in 2nd of 2ch – 15 sts.

7th to 15th rounds: As 4th round.

Stuff arm and continue to stuff as you go.

16th round: 2ch, [htr2tog] 7 times, slst in 2nd of 2ch – 8 sts. Fasten off.

Gather top edge, pull up tightly and secure.

Sew tops of arms to sides of body at shoulder position.

MUZZLE

With 5.00 hook and one strand of Cuddles and one strand of 4ply together, make 2ch.

1st round: 6htr in 2nd ch, slst in first htr.

2nd round: 2ch, 1htr in base of 2ch, [2htr in next st] 5 times, slst in 2nd of 2ch – 12 sts.

3rd round: 2ch, [1htr in next st] to end, slst in 2nd of 2ch.

4th round: 2ch, 1htr in base of 2ch, [1htr in next st, 2htr in next st] 5 times, 1htr in last st, slst in 2nd of 2ch – 18 sts.

Fasten off.

Stuff muzzle and sew to front of head.

With Light Brown and satin stitch, embroider eyes on head and nose on muzzle.

EARS (MAKE 2)

With 5.00 hook and one strand of Cuddles and one strand of 4ply together, make 2ch.

1st round: 6htr in 2nd ch, slst in first htr.

2nd round: 2ch, 1htr in base of 2ch, [2htr in next st] 5 times, slst in 2nd of 2ch – 12 sts.

3rd round: 2ch, 1htr in base of 2ch, [1htr in next st, 2htr in next st] 5 times, 1htr in last st, slst in 2nd of 2ch – 18 sts.

4th and 5th rounds: 2ch, [1htr in next st] to end, slst in 2nd of 2ch. Fasten off.

Flatten ears and over sew fastened off edge. Sew this edge to top of head.

SCARF

Beginning and ending 2cm from end, join tartan strip along long end. Fray ends of scarf by pulling out horizontal threads to create fringing. Wrap scarf round teddy's neck and tie.

PATTERN NOTES

• Yarn amounts are based on average requirements and are therefore approximate. Instructions in square brackets are worked as stated after 2nd bracket.

These sweet decorations are bound to please!

Come For Tea!

Gather together friends and family for an Easter afternoon celebration – and set the scene with our charming cakes

DIFFICULTY

✂ ✂ ✂ ✂

WHAT YOU NEED
- 3.00 crochet hook
- Pipe cleaners for stems and leaves

· Rico Design Essentials Cotton DK
Colour 1: 1x 50g (130m) Lemon (62)
Colour 2: 1 x 50g (130m) Banana (63)
Colour 3: 1 x 50g (130m) Grass Green (66)

ABBREVIATIONS

Ch, chain; st, stitch; dc, double crochet; tr, treble; ttr, triple treble; htr, half treble; dtr, double treble; slst, slip stitch.

DAFFODILS
FLOWER

Trumpet: 1st round: With 3.00 hook and Lemon make slip ring as follows: wind yarn round index finger of left hand to a form ring, insert hook into ring, yarn over hook and pull through, 1ch (does not count as a st throughout), work 6dc in ring, slst in first dc, pull end of yarn tightly to close ring – 6dc.

2nd round: 1ch, [2dc in next dc] to end, slst in first dc – 12dc.

3rd round: 1ch, [2dc in next dc, 1dc in next dc] to end, slst in first dc, turn – 18dc.

4th round: 1ch, [working in back loop only, work 1dc in next dc] to end, slst in first dc.

5th to 7th rounds: 1ch, [1dc in next dc] to end, slst in first dc.

9th round: [3ch, miss next dc, slst in next dc] to end, working slst on last repeat in base of 3ch at beginning. Fasten off.

Petals: With 3.00 hook and last round of trumpet facing, join Lemon to any free loop on 3rd round, 2ch, work 1dc and 1htr in first dc, [* work 1tr, 1dtr and 1ttr all in next dc, 3ch, slst in 3rd ch from hook, work 1ttr, 1dtr and 1tr all in next dc *, work 1htr, 1dc, and 1htr all in next dc] 5 times, then work from * to *, slst in 2nd of 2ch. Fasten off.

Stem: With 3.00 hook and Grass Green, make 36ch.

1st row: 1dc in 2nd ch from hook, [1dc in next ch] to end, turn – 35dc.

2nd and 3rd rows: 1ch, [1dc in next st] to end, and turn.

Fasten off.

Fold pipe cleaner in half and fold in sharp ends, then sew stem around pipe cleaner. Catch row-ends together at both ends.

Sew one end of stem to daffodil.

LEAF

With 3.00 hook and Grass Green, make 71ch.

1st row: 1dc in 2nd ch from hook, [1dc in next ch] to end, turn – 70dc.

2nd and 3rd rows: 1ch, [1dc in next st] to end, turn. Fasten off.

Fold in sharp ends on pipe cleaner then sew in leaf around pipe cleaner. Catch row-ends together at each end, then fold leaf in half and join ends. Sew leaf to daffodil as shown in photo.

Work an assortment of daffodils in Lemon and Banana, and make others using one shade for trumpet and other for petals.

Make leaves for some of the daffodils, and just stems for others.

DIFFICULTY

✕ ✕ ✕ ✕

WHAT YOU NEED
- 3.00 crochet hook
- Pipe cleaners for stem

- Rico Design Baby Cotton Soft DK
  (50% cotton, 50% acrylic)
  Colour 1: 1x 50g (125m) White (018)
  Colour 2: 1 x 50g (125m) Orchid (042)
  Colour 3: 1 x 50g (125m) Yellow (019)
  Colour 4: 1 x 50g (125m) Melon (020)

Colour 5: 1 x 50g (125m) Fuchsia (021)
Colour 6: 1 x 50g (125m) Emerald (032)

ABBREVIATIONS
Ch, chain; st, stitch; dc, double crochet; tr, treble; htr,
half treble; dtr, double treble; slst, slip stitch

ASSORTED SPRING FLOWERS
STEM

With 3.00 hook and Emerald, make 36ch.

1st row: 1dc in 2nd ch from hook, [1dc in next ch] to end, turn – 35dc.

2nd and 3rd rows: 1ch (does not count as a st), [1dc in next st] to end, turn.
Fasten off.

Fold pipe cleaner in half, then fold in sharp ends and sew stem around pipe
cleaner. Join row-ends at base of stem, leaving other end open.

PETALS

With 3.00 hook, join in first chosen shade to open end of pipe cleaner and
continue thus:

1st round: 1ch (does not count as a st throughout), work 2dc in each row-end of

stem, slst in first dc – 6dc.

2nd round: 1ch, [2dc in next dc, 1dc in next dc] 3 times, slst in first dc – 9dc.

3rd round: 1ch, [2dc in next dc, 1dc in each of next 2dc] 3 times, slst in first dc,
turn – 12dc.

Fasten off.

Join in second chosen shade.

4th round: [Work 1dc, 1htr, 1tr and 1dtr all in next dc, work 1dtr, 1tr, 1htr and 1dc
all in next dc] 6 times, slst in first dc.

Fasten off and neaten ends.

Working all stems in Emerald, make an assortment of spring flowers in remaining
shades.

DIFFICULTY

✕ ✕ ✕ ✕

WHAT YOU NEED

• 3.50 crochet hook
• Toy stuffing
• Stout card
• Double-sided sticky tape

• Rico Design Baby Cotton Soft DK
(50% cotton, 50% acrylic)
Colour 1: 1x 50g (125m) Snow White (018)
Colour 2: 1 x 50g (125m) Orchid (042)
Colour 3: 1 x 50g (125m) Yellow (019)
Colour 4: 1 x 50g (125m) Melon (020)
Colour 5: 1 x 50g (125m) Fuchsia (021)
Colour 6: 1 x 50g (125m) Emerald (032)

MEASUREMENTS

Approximately 7cm/2¾in diameter and 9cm/3½in
high.

ABBREVIATIONS

Ch, chain; dc, double crochet; htr, half
treble; tr, treble; slst, slip st.

CUPCAKES

BASE

1st round: With 3.50 hook and main colour, make slip ring as follows: wind yarn round index finger of left hand to form ring, insert hook into ring, yarn over hook and pull through, 2ch (does not count as a st throughout), work 8htr in ring, slst in first htr, pull end of yarn tightly to close ring.

2nd round: 2ch, [2htr in next st] 8 times, slst in top of 2ch – 16 sts.

3rd round: 2ch, [2htr in next st, 1htr in next st] 8 times, slst in top of 2ch – 24 sts.

4th round: 2ch, [2htr in next st, 1htr in each of next 2 sts] 8 times, slst in top of 2ch – 32 sts.

5th round: 2ch, [2htr in next st, 1htr in each of next 3 sts] 8 times, slst in top of 2ch – 40 sts.

6th round: 2ch, working in back loop only of every st, [1htr in next st] to end, slst in top of 2ch.

7th to 9th rounds: 2ch, [1htr in next st] to end, slst in top of 2ch.

Fasten off.

TOP

1st round: With 3.50 hook and main colour, make slip ring as on base, 2ch (does not count as a st throughout), work 8htr in ring, slst in first htr, pull end of yarn tightly to close ring.

2nd round: 2ch, working in back loop only of every st, [2htr in next st] 8 times, slst in top of 2ch – 16 sts.

3rd round: 2ch, [1htr in next st] to end, slst in top of 2ch.

4th round: 2ch, working in back loop only of every st, [2htr in next st, 1htr in next st] 8 times, slst in top of 2ch – 24 sts.

5th round: As 3rd round.

6th round: 2ch, working in back loop only of every st, [2htr in next st, 1htr in each of next 2 sts] 8 times, slst in top of 2ch – 32 sts.

7th round: As 3rd round.

8th round: 2ch, working in back loop of every st only, [2htr in next st, 1htr in each of next 3 sts] 8 times, slst in top of 2ch – 40 sts.

9th round: As 3rd round.

Fasten off.

ICING

First layer: With right side facing and using 3.50 hook, join contrast colour with slst to front loop of any st on 1st round of top, 5tr in next st – shell made, [slst in next st, 5tr in next st] to end, slst in first slst – 4 shells.

Fasten off.

Second layer: With right side facing and using 3.50 hook, join contrast colour with slst to front loop of any st on 3rd round of top, 5tr in next st, [slst in next st, 5tr in next st] to end, slst in first slst – 8 shells.

Fasten off.

Third layer: With right side facing and using 3.50 hook, join contrast colour with slst to front loop of any st on 5th round of top, miss next st, 5tr in next st, miss next st, [slst in next st, miss next st, 5tr in next st, miss next st] to end, slst in first slst – 6 shells.

Fasten off.

Fourth layer: With right side facing and using 3.50 hook, join contrast colour with slst to front loop of any st on 7th round of top, miss next st, 5tr in next st, miss next st, [slst in next st, miss next st, 5tr in next st, miss next st] to end, slst in first slst – 8 shells.

Fasten off.

Fifth layer: With right side facing and using 3.50 hook, join contrast colour with slst to any st on 9th round of top, miss next st, 5tr in next st, miss next st, [slst in next st, miss next st, 5tr in next st, miss next st] to end, slst in first slst – 10 shells.

Fasten off.

TO COMPLETE

Cut circle in stout card to fit base of cake. Using double sided sticky tape, stick the card to inside of base. Sew bottom to last round of top under last layer of icing, leaving an opening. Stuff firmly and close the opening.

Super Toys

Three cuddly characters with extra-special powers...

DIFFICULTY

✕ ✕ ✕ ✕

WHAT YOU NEED

- 4.00 crochet hook
- Washable toy stuffing
- DMC Woolly (100% wool)

BAT BUNNY:

Colour 1: 1x 50g (125m) Grey (122)

Colour 2: 1 x 50g (125m) Peach (101)

Colour 3: 1 x 50g (125m) Charcoal (123)

Colour 4: 1 x 50g (125m) Yellow (093)

Colour 5: Oddment Cream (03)

SUPER PUP:

Colour 1: 1x 50g (125m) Teal (077)

Colour 2: 1 x 50g (125m) Grey (122)

Colour 3: 1 x 50g (125m) Red (103)

Colour 4: 1 x 50g (125m) Yellow (093)

Colour 5: Oddment Cream (03)

Colour 6: Oddment Charcoal (123)

WONDER BEAR:

Colour 1: 1 x 50g (125m) Peach (101)

Colour 2: 1 x 50g (125m) Red (103)

Colour 3: 1 x 50g (125m) Teal (077)

Colour 4: 1 x 50g (125m) Yellow (093)

Colour 5: Oddment Cream (03)

Colour 6: Oddment Charcoal (123)

MEASUREMENTS

Approximately 23cm/9in tall, excluding ears.

ABBREVIATIONS

Ch, chain; dc, double crochet; st, stitch; tr, treble; slst, slip stitch; dc2tog, work 2dc together thus: [insert hook in next st, yarn round hook and pull through] twice, yarn round hook and pull through all 3 loops on hook.

BAT BUNNY
BODY & LEGS

Body: 1st round: With 4.00 hook and Grey, make slip ring as follows: wind yarn round index finger of left hand to form ring, insert hook into ring, yarn over hook and pull through, 1ch (does not count as st), work 6dc in ring, pull end of yarn tightly to close ring. Mark end of last round and move this marker up at end of every round.

2nd round: [2dc in next st] 6 times – 12 sts.

3rd round: [2dc in next st, 1dc in next st] 6 times – 18 sts.

4th round: [2dc in next st, 1dc in each of next 2 sts] 6 times – 24 sts.

5th round: [2dc in next st, 1dc in each of next 3 sts] 6 times – 30 sts.

6th round: [2dc in next st, 1dc in each of next 4 sts] 6 times – 36 sts.

7th round: [1dc in next st] to end.

8th to 12th rounds: As 7th round.

13th round: [2dc in next st, 1dc in each of next 5 sts] 6 times – 42 sts.

14th to 19th rounds: As 7th round.

20th round: [2dc in next st, 1dc in each of next 6 sts] 6 times – 48 sts.

21st to 26th rounds: As 7th round.

Dividing round: 1dc in each of first 24 sts. Work in rounds on these 24 sts only for first leg.

First leg: Work 15 rounds as 7th round.

Slst in back loop of next st.

Next round: Working in back loop only of every st, 1ch (does not count as a st), 1dc in same place as slst, 1dc in next st, dc2tog, [1dc in each of next 2 sts, dc2tog] 5 times, slst in 1ch – 18 sts.

Next round: [1dc in next st, dc2tog] 6 times – 12 sts. Fasten off.

Second leg: Rejoin yarn to end of dividing round, 1dc in each of 24 sts.

Work 15 rounds as 7th round.

Slst in back loop of next st.

Next round: Working in back loop only of every st, 1ch (does not count as a st), 1dc in same place as slst, 1dc in next st, dc2tog, [1dc in each of next 2 sts, dc2tog] 5 times, slst in 1ch – 18 sts.

Next round: [1dc in next st, dc2tog] 6 times – 12 sts. Fasten off.

Stuff body and legs firmly. Gather fastened-off edge on each leg, pull up tightly and secure.

HEAD

1st round: With 4.00 hook and Peach, make slip ring as on body and legs, 1ch (does not count as st), work 6dc in ring, pull end of yarn tightly to close ring. Mark end of last round and move this marker up at end of every round.

2nd round: [2dc in next st] 6 times – 12 sts.

3rd round: [2dc in next st, 1dc in next st] 6 times – 18 sts.

4th round: [2dc in next st, 1dc in each of next 2 sts] 6 times – 24 sts.

5th round: [2dc in next st, 1dc in each of next 3 sts] 6 times – 30 sts.

6th round: [2dc in next st, 1dc in each of next 4 sts] 6 times – 36 sts.

7th round: [2dc in next st, 1dc in each of next 5 sts] 6 times – 42 sts.

8th round: [2dc in next st, 1dc in each of next 6 sts] 6 times – 48 sts.

9th round: [1dc in next st] to end.

10th to 14th rounds: As 9th round.

15th round: [Dc2tog, 1dc in each of next 6 sts] 6 times – 42 sts.

16th round: [Dc2tog, 1dc in each of next 5 sts] 6 times – 36 sts.

17th round: [Dc2tog, 1dc in each of next 4 sts] 6 times – 30 sts.

18th round: [Dc2tog, 1dc in each of next 3 sts] 6 times – 24 sts.

19th round: [Dc2tog, 1dc in each of next 2 sts] 6 times – 18 sts.

20th round: [Dc2tog, 1dc in next st] 6 times – 12 sts. Fasten off.

Stuff head firmly and sew to top of body.

ARMS (MAKE 2)

1st round: With 4.00 hook and Peach, make slip ring as on body and legs, 1ch (does not count as st), work 6dc in ring, pull end of yarn tightly to close ring. Mark end of last round and move this marker up at end of every round.

2nd round: [2dc in next st] 6 times – 12 sts.

3rd round: [2dc in next st, 1dc in next st] 6 times – 18 sts.

4th round: [1dc in next st] to end.

5th round: As 4th round.

Change to Grey.

6th round: As 4th round.

7th round: [Dc2tog, 1dc in each of next 4 sts] 3 times – 15 sts.

8th to 17th rounds: As 4th round.

18th round: [Dc2tog, 1dc in each of next 3 sts] 3 times – 12 sts.

19th to 24th rounds: As 4th round. Fasten off.

Stuff lower part of arms firmly, easing stuffing along towards top. Flatten top edge and sew in position.

SHORTS

With 4.00 hook and Charcoal, make 48ch, slst in first ch to form a ring, making sure that the chain is not twisted.

1st round: [1dc in next ch] to end.

Mark end of last round and move this marker up at end of every round.

2nd round: [1dc in next st] to end.

3rd to 7th rounds: As 2nd round.

Dividing round: 1dc in each of first 24 sts. Work in rounds on these 24 sts only for first leg.

First leg: Work 2 rounds as 2nd round.

Slst in next dc and fasten off.

Second leg: Rejoin yarn to end of dividing round, 1dc in each of 24 sts.

Work 2 rounds as 2nd round.

Slst in next dc and fasten off.

Place shorts on body and stitch in position along top edge.

With 4.00 hook, Yellow an inserting hook around stitches on body, work 1 round of dc above the top edge of shorts.

Slst in first dc and fasten off.

MASK

1st round: With 4.00 hook and Charcoal, make slip ring as on body and legs, 1ch (does not count as st), work 6dc in ring, pull end of yarn tightly to close ring.

Mark end of last round and move this marker up at end of every round.

2nd round: [2dc in next st] 6 times – 12 sts.

3rd round: [2dc in next st, 1dc in next st] 6 times – 18 sts.

4th round: [2dc in next st, 1dc in each of next 2 sts] 6 times – 24 sts.

5th round: [2dc in next st, 1dc in each of next 3 sts] 6 times – 30 sts.

6th round: [2dc in next st, 1dc in each of next 4 sts] 6 times – 36 sts.

7th round: [2dc in next st, 1dc in each of next 5 sts] 6 times – 42 sts.

8th round: [2dc in next st, 1dc in each of next 6 sts] 6 times – 48 sts.

9th round: [2dc in next st, 1dc in each of next 7 sts] 6 times – 54 sts.

10th to 18th rounds: [1dc in next st] to end.

Slst in first dc and fasten off.

Place mask on head and secure in position.

EARS (MAKE 2)

1st round: With 4.00 hook and Charcoal, make slip ring as on body and legs, 1ch (does not count as st), work 6dc in ring, pull end of yarn tightly to close ring.

Mark end of last round and move this marker up at end of every round.

2nd round: [2dc in next st] 6 times – 12 sts.

3rd round: [2dc in next st, 1dc in next st] 6 times – 18 sts.

4th round: [1dc in next st] to end.

5th and 6th rounds: As 4th round.

7th round: [Dc2tog, 1dc in each of next 4 sts] 3 times – 15 sts.

8th and 9th rounds: As 4th round.

10th round: [Dc2tog, 1dc in each of next 3 sts] 3 times – 12 sts.

11th to 18th rounds: As 4th round.

Slst in first dc and fasten off.

Flatten fastened-off edge and sew through both layers to top of head.

EYES (MAKE 2)

1st round: With 4.00 hook and Cream, make slip ring as on body and legs, 1ch (does not count as st), work 6dc in ring, pull end of yarn tightly to close ring.

2nd round: 2dc in each of first 3 sts, slst in next st. Fasten off.

Sew eyes in position. With Charcoal, work V stitch on each eye for pupil.

With Charcoal, embroider mouth as shown in photo.

CHEST MOTIF

With 4.00 hook and Yellow, make 5ch.

1st round: 1dc in 2nd ch from hook, 1dc in each of next 2ch, 3dc in last ch, then work along other side of ch thus: 1dc in each of next 2ch, 2dc in last ch – 10 sts.

2nd round: 1dc in each of next 4dc, 3dc in next dc, 1dc in of each of next 4dc, 3dc in last dc – 14 sts.

3rd round: 1dc in each of next 4dc, 2dc in each of next 3dc, 1dc in of each of next 4dc, 2dc in each of last 3dc – 20 sts.

Slst in first dc and fasten off.

Place motif on front of body and sew in position. With Charcoal, embroider symbol of flying bird at centre of motif.

CAPE

With 4.00 hook and Charcoal, make 22ch.

1st row: 1tr in 3rd ch from hook (counts as 2 sts), [1tr in next ch] to end, turn – 21 sts.

2nd to 17th rows: 3ch, [1tr in next st] to end, turn.

Next round: Work 1 round of dc evenly along all sides, working 3dc in each corner. Slst in first dc and fasten off.

Fold over last 2 rows along one short end and wrap this edge round back of neck and shoulders, then secure in position.

SUPER PUP
BODY & LEGS

Using Teal, work as Bat Bunny.

HEAD

Using Grey, work as Bat Bunny.

ARMS (MAKE 2)

Using Grey instead of Peach and Teal instead of Grey, work as Bat Bunny.

SHORTS

Using Red instead of Charcoal and Teal instead of Yellow, work as Bat Bunny.

EARS (MAKE 2)

1st round: With 4.00 hook and Grey, make slip ring as on body and legs, 1ch (does not count as st), work 6dc in ring, pull end of yarn tightly to close ring. Mark end of last round and move this marker up at end of every round.

2nd round: [2dc in next st, 1dc in next st] 3 times – 9 sts.

3rd and 4th rounds: [1dc in next st] to end.

5th round: [2dc in next st, 1dc in each of next 2 sts] 3 times – 12 sts.

6th round: [2dc in next st, 1dc in next st] 6 times, slst in first dc – 18 sts. Fasten off.

Flatten fastened-off edge and sew through both layers to top of head. Tip ears forward slightly and catch first layer to head.

EYE PATCH

1st round: With 4.00 hook and Charcoal, make slip ring as on body and legs, 1ch (does not count as st), work 6dc in ring, pull end of yarn tightly to close ring.

2nd round: [2dc in next st] 6 times – 12 sts.

3rd round: [2dc in next st, 1dc in next st] 6 times – 18 sts. Fasten off.

EYES (MAKE 2)

Work as Bat Bunny.

Position eyes on head, then place eye patch slightly under right eye and to the back of head and sew them on securely. With Charcoal, work V stitch on each eye for pupil.

With Charcoal embroider mouth as shown in photo.

CHEST MOTIF

1st round: With 4.00 hook and Yellow, make slip ring as on body and legs, 1ch (does not count as st), 12dc into ring, slst in first dc, pull end of yarn tightly to close ring.

2nd round: 1ch (does not count as st), [1dc in each of next 3dc, 3dc in next dc] 3 times – 18 sts.

3rd round: 1dc in each of first 4dc, 3dc in next dc, [1dc in each of next 5dc, 3dc in next dc] twice, 1dc in last dc, slst in first dc – 24 sts. Fasten off. Place motif on front of body and sew in position. With Charcoal, embroider letter S at centre of motif.

CAPE

With Red, work as Bat Bunny.

WONDER BEAR
BODY & LEGS

Work as Bat Bunny, working 1st to 11th rounds in Peach, 12th to 26th rounds in Red, complete in Peach.

HEAD

Work as Bat Bunny.

ARMS (MAKE 2)

Work as Bat Bunny, working 1st to 18th rounds in Red and 19th to 24th rounds in Peach.

SHORTS

Using Teal instead of Charcoal and Red instead of Yellow, work as Bat bunny.

With 4.00 hook and Yellow, work row of dc as before above first round of Red on body, taking dc 2 rounds down at centre of front to form cleavage.

Slst in first dc and fasten off.

EARS (MAKE 2)

1st round: With 4.00 hook and Peach, make slip ring as on body and head, 1ch (does not count as st), work 6dc in ring, pull end of yarn tightly to close ring. Mark end of last round and move this marker up at end of every round.

2nd round: [2dc in next st] 6 times – 12 sts.

3rd round: [2dc in next st, 1dc in each of next 3 sts] 6 times – 15 sts.

4th round: [1dc in next st] to end, slst in first dc. Fasten off.

Flatten fastened-off edge, curve this edge slightly and sew through both layers to top of head.

HEAD BAND

With 4.00 hook and Yellow, make 54ch, slst in first ch to form a ring, making sure that the chain is not twisted.

1st round: [1dc in next ch] to end, slst in first dc. Fasten off.

Place headband on head and secure in position. With Red, embroider motif at centre front.

EYES (MAKE 2)

Work as Bat Bunny.

CAPE

With Yellow, work as Bat Bunny.